Foreword:
The Father of the Constitution

The title of this book is a misnomer. The charter of government that has guided the destinies of the United States for 177 years was not created entirely by Mr. Madison. But few important documents are attributable entirely to the one man with whom they may be associated. Alexander Hamilton and James Madison wrote more of Washington's Farewell Address than Washington did; John Quincy Adams wrote at least as much of the Monroe Doctrine as Monroe did; even Thomas Jefferson, although he personally wrote the first draft of the Declaration of Independence, leaned heavily on Montesquieu, John Locke, James Mason, and others for his ideas. So it is not too farfetched to refer to the Constitution as Mr. Madison's; if any man is worthy of the title "Father of the Constitu-

v

tion," that man is Madison. He contributed more to the precious document than anybody else.

Madison was best described by his future wife, the lively widow Dolly Payne Todd, when, after their first meeting, she referred to him as "the great little Madison." Short, almost fragile of figure, retiring in manner, sober in dress, and with a modesty that made him shy, Madison was the antithesis of the hard-riding, hard-drinking, cock-fighting, gambling Virginia planter aristocracy to which he was born. A bookworm from boyhood, he was so engrossed, at Princeton, with history, the classics, the philosophers, and especially the philosophy of government, that he spent but three hours a night in bed, a regime that left his health so impaired that he was unsuited for service in the field during the Revolution.

Madison was not one of the heroic champions of freedom and democracy. Rather, he was the scholar and statesman of the reform. During his twenties, when he served on the Virginia Constitutional Convention and in the Virginia legislature he was a disciple of the older Virginian, his good friend Thomas Jefferson. Madison was one of the most influential members of the Continental Congress during the last four years of the war and its unquestioned authority on the history of republican government. Back in the Virginia legislature after the war, he secured the passage of that state's famed statute for religious freedom, a pet project of Jefferson's.

Through the early postwar years he labored for a stronger central government, thrusting aside his shyness to dispute Patrick Henry, the powerful Lees, and other Virginia statesmen when they refused to give Congress the right to raise revenue. He was the leader in the preliminary steps that brought the Constitutional Convention into being: the Mount Vernon Conference and the Annapolis Convention. In fact, it was at his suggestion that Virginia proposed a convention of the thirteen states to consider revision of the Articles of Confederation. He was the chief author of the Virginia Plan, which Edmund Randolph presented to the Constitutional Convention and which was the base from which they started to work. During the entire convention he never missed a session and was deeply involved in every important decision that the body made.

Of Madison's contribution to the Constitution Max Farrand, one of the leading modern authorities on the document, wrote: "When one studies the contemporary conditions, and tries to discover how well the men of that time grasped the situation; and when one goes farther and, in the light of our subsequent knowledge, seeks to learn how wise were the remedies they proposed, Madison stands preeminent. He seems to have lacked imagination, but this very lack made his work of peculiar value at the moment. His remedies for the unsatisfactory state of affairs under the Confederation, were not founded on theoretical speculations, they were practical. They were in accord with the historical development of our country and in keeping with the genius of our institutions. The evidence is also strong that Madison not only took an important part in the debates but that he was actually looked up to by both friends and opponents as the leader of those in the Convention who were in favor of a strong national government."

In addition to all of this he performed one other service that bears on his title as "Father of the Constitution." In all of his study of "the history of the most distinguished confederacies, particularly those of antiquity, more especially in what related to the processes, the principles, the reasons and the anticipations which prevailed in the formation of them," he had been impeded by the absence of authentic records. He was determined that posterity would not have this difficulty in connection with the formation of the government of the United States and decided to keep a personal record of all that happened at the Convention. He later wrote:

"I chose a seat in front of the presiding member, with the other members on my right and left hand. In this favorable position for hearing all that passed I noted in terms legible and in abbreviations and marks intelligible to myself what was read from the chair or spoken by the members; and losing not a moment unnecessarily between the adjournment and the reassembling of the Convention, I was enabled to write out my daily notes during the session, or within a few finishing days after its close in the extent and form preserved, in my own hand. . . . I was not absent a single day, nor more than a casual fraction of an hour in any day, so that I cannot have lost a single speech, except a short one."

Some other members kept skimpy and casual notes; and there was an official journal—for what it was worth. But if Madison had not so ably performed his self-imposed chore —which, he later said, "almost killed me,"—there would be nothing even approaching a complete record of the creation of the most important charter of government in world history.

MR. MADISON'S CONSTITUTION

MR. MADISON'S CONSTITUTION

THE STORY BEHIND THE CONSTITUTIONAL CONVENTION

By Frank Donovan

ILLUSTRATED

DODD, MEAD & COMPANY

NEW YORK

Library of Congress Catalog Card Number: 65-17612

Printed in the United States of America
by Vail-Ballou Press, Inc., Binghamton, N.Y.

Contents

Illustrations

Following page 52

1

The Ineffectual Articles

If roaring cheers, thundering salutes, grandiloquent speeches, and pretty girls tossing flowers were a true indication, George Washington could look forward to an easy time as first President of the United States. His Excellency did not think so. As the white horses drew his carriage between lines of madly enthusiastic onlookers en route to his inauguration in New York in April, 1789, the ex-General was somewhat disturbed and confused.

He was about to become the chief executive of a nation that had just adopted a new and unique charter of government. Maybe it would work; but there were many who had grave doubts. Alexander Hamilton, who had labored lustily to secure its ratification, privately affirmed that the new Constitution was a "frail and worthless fabric" that would not last over ten years. Although there was much that Thomas Jefferson liked in the new charter, he was dubious and told James Madison, "I hope you will not be discouraged from other trials, if the present one should fail of its full effect." Benjamin Franklin, who helped to draft the charter and whose great influence, along with Washington's, was a prime factor in securing its ratification, had said as he signed the document, "I confess that I do not entirely approve of this Constitution at present." And he had added, in connection with its permanence, "In this world nothing can be said to be certain but death and taxes."

These were men who, in general, approved of remodeling the central government. Others, of almost equal stature, opposed the whole idea. Samuel Adams and John Hancock, earliest and staunchest of the Revolution leaders, were among these; as was Richard Henry Lee, who had offered the resolution for independence. Patrick Henry condemned the Constitution by saying, "I look on that paper as the most fatal plan that could possibly be conceived to enslave a free people."

Most thinking men realized that the Constitution was not a logical, coolly contrived, and carefully planned charter of government. It was a bundle of compromises designed to placate extremists at both ends; the little states and big ones, the nationalists and state's righters, the creditors and the debtors, the merchants and the farmers, the conservatives and the radicals, the North and the South. Only wise old Benjamin Franklin seemed to recognize that compromise would always be the very essence of democratic government.

The problem was that, to this time, the United States had been united in little except their dislike for British rule and their enthusiasm for George Washington. In fact, if one wants to split hairs, Washington would be the chief executive in only eleven states; North Carolina had not yet ratified the Constitution, and little Rhode Island was loudly proclaiming that she never would. The 3,929,000 souls—including 757,000 Negroes—who inhabited the long coastal strip east of the Allegheny Mountains from New Hampshire to Georgia differed in more ways than they agreed. Almost all spoke English, and most, except the Negroes, were Protestants of English descent. They had that much in common—along with a love for personal liberty which was expressed in a rugged individualism that engendered diversity rather than conformity.

The Connecticut Yankee in his stony northern fields did not see eye to eye with the North Carolinian on his soft southern loam. The shrewd merchant and trader of Massachusetts had little in common with the languid planter of tidewater Virginia. Americans on different sections of the coast had grown up under different social and religious systems and each favored his own. They had vastly different local problems, which they were loath to subordinate to the common good. They had started as members of thirteen separate and distinct British colonies, each jealous of its own prerogatives. When the colonies became states, the jealousy remained. Americans were citizens of states, not of a nation.

And most of the people of the United States had one more thing in common: their dislike for government—all government except that which was purely local. This had led them to unite in throwing off the oppressive yoke of British rule. But after their rebellion was successful they distrusted any national government that might be oppressive of what they considered their individual and communal rights.

From the earliest days the colonies had united temporarily when danger threatened. In 1643 the New England Confederation had been formed for protection against the Indians and, to a lesser extent, the French and the Dutch. There followed frequent proposals for unity against a common danger; the best known was that presented by Franklin to the Albany Congress of 1754. The Stamp Act Congress had met in 1765, at the beginning of the serious trouble with Great Britain. And finally the Continental Congress had presided over the opening act in the rebellion.

This Congress recognized that some form of central government was necessary in order to carry on the war with Britain. Immediately after Richard Henry Lee made the proposal "that these colonies are and of a right ought to be free and independent states," on June 7, 1776, Congress had appointed two committees. One was to draft a Declaration of Independence to be released when and if Lee's motion was passed. The other, headed by John Dickinson of Pennsylvania, was ordered to prepare the articles of union.

Jefferson's immortal document was immediately accepted when presented by the first committee, but the Articles of Confederation submitted by Dickinson's committee a few days later were the subject of intermittent bickering in Congress for sixteen months and were not ratified by the states until March 1, 1781. During the War Congress functioned, when it did function, as though the Articles were in effect, but the charter of government did not become legally effective until the fighting was almost over. Meanwhile the individual states had adopted constitutions that, except for preambles that enunciated certain general principles of government philosophy and political morality, differed little from the systems of government under which the states had operated as colonies.

It seems evident that Dickinson's committee took Franklin's plan for union of 1754 as a starting point and revised, enlarged, and brought it up to date as the Articles of Confederation. Important sections of the Articles are found, in some cases word for word, in Franklin's proposal. Since Franklin's plan was conceived primarily to meet a specific situation, it was not necessarily the ideal basis for a permanent charter of government; and it is unlikely that Dickinson's committee anticipated that their proposal would be more than a wartime measure.

The Articles of Confederation established, in Article III, a "firm league of friendship" between the states for their "common defense, the security of their liberties, and their mutual and general welfare." There were thirteen articles in all, and they presumably gave Congress all necessary powers to carry on the war and operate some essential domestic services. The Congress could declare war and make peace; raise an army and build a navy; borrow money; make treaties; appoint courts to judge pirates; maintain a common treasury to pay for the war, carry the mails, coin money, deal with the Indians, and much more.

On the face of it these seem to be broad powers, but buried in Article IX, without even a title of its own, was the joker. The paragraph read: "The United States in Congress assembled shall never engage in war, nor grant letters of marque and reprisal in time of peace, nor enter into any treaties or alliances, nor coin money, nor regulate the value thereof, nor ascertain the sums and expense necessary for the defense and welfare of the United States, or any of them, nor emit bills, nor borrow money on the credit of the United States, nor appropriate money, nor agree upon the number of vessels of war to be built or purchased, nor the number of land and sea forces to be raised, nor appoint a commander-in-chief of the army and navy, unless nine States assent to the same."

In short, Congress could do virtually nothing without the express approval of two thirds of the states. Since each state, regardless of size or population, had a single vote in the Congress, the four New England States, plus New York or New Jersey, or the four southern states, plus Maryland or Delaware—or any 5 states—could prevent the national government from functioning.

Article XIII provided that "Every State shall abide by the determinations of the United States in Congress assembled." But nowhere did the Articles of Confederation give the federal government power to compel obedience. Any state that disapproved of a Congressional resolution that was endorsed by nine other states could—and did—ignore it with impunity.

The third fault with the Articles of Confederation as a charter of government was that they could not be amended except by the unanimous approval of the states. For all practical purposes the so-called United States was a league of sovereign republics banded together for a limited purpose. That purpose did not include the formation of a nation.

The most immediately apparent defect of the Confederacy was the lack of any power to raise money by taxation. The Articles provided that the national treasury "should be supplied by the several states, in proportion to the value of land within each State, granted to or surveyed for any person." But, as with all else, each state honored the requisitions of Congress only to the extent it saw fit.

There has never been a reasonable explanation of how the United States supported a war for six years with worthless paper currency and a dollop of borrowed gold. Such intangibles as faith, dedication, and patriotism triumphed over reasonable economics. But when the fighting ended, these factors ceased to apply. In the two years between the end of active hostilities at Yorktown in 1781 and the Treaty of Paris in 1783, Congress asked the states for $10,-000,000. It received $1,500,000. When William Morris resigned as Superintendent of Finance in 1784, there was $21,000 in the national treasury. At no time during the immediate postwar years were the national revenues equal to the interest on the national debt.

All efforts of Congress to correct this came to naught. In 1781 they proposed that the Articles be amended to authorize a national tax of 5 per cent on imports and goods condemned in prize cases. Twelve states agreed; Rhode Island said no. In 1783 Congress again proposed certain taxes, plus an annual contribution of $1,500,000 from the states, to be apportioned on the basis of population instead of land. This time, after a three-year delay, New York said no.

John Fiske, in his *Critical Period of American History*, wrote: "The period of five years following the peace of 1783 was the most critical moment in all the history of the American people. The dangers from which we were saved in 1788 were even greater than were the dangers from which we were saved in 1865." This was, perhaps, an exaggeration. In 1861 secession was a fact. In 1786 dissolution was merely imminent; but few informed observers believed that the newly independent states would long be held together as a nation by what Washington called the "rope of sand" that constituted their charter of government.

Congress was, for the most part, ignored. Many of the delegates were admittedly second-rate men. The giants of the Revolution were dispersed. Washington and Franklin had retired, Jefferson, Adams, and Jay were abroad. Most top-ranking leaders were serving their respective states at home in positions they considered more important than national service. Weeks, sometimes months, passed during which the national legislature could not meet because there was not a quorum.

James Madison summarized the situation by writing to Virginia's Govenor Edmund Randolph: "Our situation is becoming every day more and more critical. No money comes into the federal treasury; no respect is paid to the federal authority; and people of reflection unanimously agree that the existing Confederacy is tottering to its foundation. Many individuals of weight, particularly in the eastern district, are suspected of leaning toward monarchy. Other individuals predict a partition of the states into two or more confederacies. It is pretty certain that if some radical amendment . . . cannot be devised and introduced, one or other of these revolutions—the latter no doubt—will take place."

The states went their not-so-merry separate ways. Most of them refused to honor the stipulation in the Treaty of Paris that Loyalists were to be compensated for property that had been confiscated during the war. This gave England a fine excuse for retaining the military posts in the

Northwest, which she had agreed to abandon, a situation that ultimately led to the War of 1812 more directly than "Free Trade and Sailors Rights."

In interstate commerce some states acted as sovereign nations toward their sister states, imposing fees, charges, and duties on domestic as well as foreign imports. James Madison wrote: "Some of the States . . . having no convenient ports for foreign commerce, were subject to be taxed by their neighbors, through whose ports their commerce was carried on. New Jersey, placed between Philadelphia and New York, was likened to a cask tapped at both ends; and North Carolina, between Virginia and South Carolina, to a patient bleeding at both arms."

Interstate relationship and lack of unity were well exemplified by John Fiske in this description of the relations between New York and her neighbors. "The city of New York, with its population of 30,000 souls, had long been supplied with firewood from Connecticut, and with butter and cheese, chickens and garden vegetables from the thrifty farms of New Jersey. This trade, it was observed, carried thousands of dollars out of the city and into the pockets of the detested Yankees and despised Jerseymen. 'It was ruinous to domestic industry,' said the men of New York. 'It must stopped by . . . a navigation act and a protective tarif.' Acts were accordingly passed, obliging every Yankee sloop which came down through Hell Gate, and every Jersey market boat which was rowed across Paulus Hook to Cortlandt Street, to pay entrance fees and obtain clearances at the custom house, just as was done by ships from London and Hamburg. . . .

"The city of New York had lately bought a small patch of ground on Sandy Hook, and had built a lighthouse there. This lighthouse was the one weak spot in the heel of Achilles where a hostile arrow could strike, and New Jersey gave vent to her indignation by laying a tax of $1,800 a year on it. Connecticut was equally prompt. At a great meeting of businessmen, held in New London, it was unanimously agreed to suspend all commercial intercourse with New York. Every merchant signed an agreement, under penalty of $250 for the first offense, not to send any goods whatever into the hated state for a period of twelve months."

Seven of the states sought to solve their fiscal problems by printing paper money. The only hard money in the country, except for coppers, was the product of foreign mints, and this was rapidly being drained off to pay for imports. Gold, in terms of dollars, had a fairly constant value, but silver pieces had not less than five separate values in different states. Rhode Island passed a law that sought to compel the merchants of that state to accept its paper money at face value. Many promptly closed their doors or sought to do business under a barter system. This led farmers to withhold food from the cities and for a time her government was in a state of anarchy.

A more serious disturbance, which led to bloodshed, was Shays' Rebellion in western Massachusetts. The farmers demanded an issue of paper money to pay their taxes and debts. When the legislature adjourned without voting it, they banded together under the leadership of a destitute farmer and ex-army captain named Daniel Shays and marched to prevent the courts from sitting to give judgments to creditors. This incipient civil war, which included an attack on the arsenal at Springfield, was suppressed by local militia. There were similar, though less violent, disturbances in other states arising from the absence of a national currency. Congress was powerless to correct the cause or interfere in the effect.

Of perhaps greater importance than money was the problem of markets. The only real wealth possessed by any of the states was in the products of nature—agricultural commodities, lumber, hides, furs, fish and so on. These would ultimately produce money if they could be sold abroad. But the Americans were surprised and resentful that their biggest customer, Great Britain, did not intend to favor them with what they considered reasonable trade privileges. Trade restrictions had been an important cause of the rebellion. After they became foreigners instead of colonists to Great Britain, the Americans—the reasoning here defies understanding—expected to be treated better. Instead, of course, trade restrictions were more severe.

The answer was retaliation by the individual states. Maryland established discriminatory rates for British shipping; South Carolina imposed a general 2½-per-cent duty on all foreign goods; Massachusetts banned the export of United States products in British ships; Pennsylvania, New York, North Carolina, New Hampshire, and Rhode Island each created separate laws to control international trade.

The Congress, in 1784, rather plaintively tried to reason with independent members of the league of states. After pointing out the importance of commerce, which affected "the fortune of every citizen," and declaring that "Great Britain had adopted regulations destructive of our commerce with the West Indian Islands," they added, "Unless the United States in Congress assembled shall be vested with powers competent to the protection of commerce,

they can never command reciprocal advantages in trade."
They proposed that the Articles of Confederation be
amended to empower Congress to adopt navigation acts.
Only two states endorsed the idea.

When Franklin, Adams, and Jefferson tried to discuss
trade concessions with the British Ambassador in Paris, he
blandly told them that his country could hardly enter into
a treaty with Congress when one state could render "to-
tally fruitless and ineffectual" any such agreement, and
advised them to secure authorization from each of the several states before attempting to make a deal. Throughout
Europe the respect that the rebellious colonists had earned
by their military success was changing to contempt for
their inability to agree among themselves. One contemporary American traveler said that his country was "held in
the same light by foreign nations as a well behaved Negro
in a gentleman's family."

Within two years after the war ended the United States
was in the trough of a severe depression, "the Panic of
1785." In 1786 conditions worsened as exports sank below
4.5 million dollars and farm wages dropped 20 per cent
below the wartime level. The danger of destitution induced many Americans to be at least receptive to the possibility of giving up some of their individual and state's
rights to support a united effort.

A few men who were more concerned for the welfare of
the United States than for that of their individual com-
monwealths and who dreamed of a great future for the
new nation were convinced that the only way to remove
the danger of dissolution was to establish a central government with some authority. Washington took time from the
affairs of his plantations to spread this gospel. He wrote

Henry Knox: "Contracted ideas, local pursuits and absurd jealousy are continually leading us from those great and fundamental principles which are characteristic of wise and powerful nations, and without which we are no more than a rope of sand and shall as easily be broken. . . . the Confederation appears to me to be a shadow without substance." And again: "If we are afraid to trust one another under qualified powers there is an end to the Union. . . . We are either a united people or we are not. If the former, let us in all matters of general concern act as a nation which has national objects to promote and a national character to support. If we are not, let us no longer act a farce of pretending to it."

Other isolated leaders expressed themselves more specifically as to the faults of the Confederacy and the steps that should be taken to correct them. James Madison expressed the view generally held by this small group in another letter to Edmund Randolph. "I hold it for a fundamental point, that an individual independence of the states is utterly irreconcilable with the idea of an aggregate sovereignty. I think, at the same time, that a consolidation of the states into one simple republic is not less unattainable than it would be inexpedient. Let it be tried, then, whether any middle ground can be taken, which will at once support a due supremacy of the national authority, and leave in force the local authorities so far as they can be subordinately useful.

"The first step to be taken is, I think, a change in the principle of representation. According to the present form of the Union, an equality of suffrage, if not just towards the larger members of it, is at least safe to them, as the liberty they exercise of rejecting or executing the acts of

Congress is uncontrollable by the nominal sovereignty of Congress. Under a system which would operate without the intervention of the states, the case would be materially altered. A vote from Delaware would have the same effect as one from Massachusetts or Virginia.

"Let the national government be armed with a positive and complete authority in all cases where uniform measures are necessary, as in trade, &c., &c. Let it also retain the powers which it now possesses.

"Let it have a negative, in all cases whatsoever, on the legislative acts of the states, as the king of Great Britain heretofore had. This I conceive to be essential, and the least possible of abridgment of the state sovereignties. Without such a defensive power, every positive power that can be given on paper will be unavailing. It will also give internal stability to the states. There has been no moment, since the peace, at which the federal assent would have been given to paper money, &c., &c.

"Let this national supremacy be extended also to the judiciary department. If the judges in the last resort depend on the states, and are bound by their oaths to them and not to the Union, the intention of the law and the interests of the nation may be defeated by the obsequiousness of the tribunals to the policy or prejudices of the states. It seems at least essential that an appeal should lie to some national tribunals in all cases which concern foreigners, or inhabitants of other states. . . .

"A government formed of such extensive powers ought to be well organized. The legislative department may be divided into two branches—one of them to be chosen every ―――― years by the legislatures, or the people at large; the other to consist of a more select number, holding their appointments for a longer term, and going out in rotation. Perhaps the negative on the state laws may be most conveniently lodged in this branch. . . .

"A national executive will also be necessary. I have scarcely ventured to form my own opinion yet, either of the manner in which it ought to be constituted, or of the authorities with which it ought to be clothed.

"An article ought to be inserted expressly guaranteeing the tranquility of the states against internal as well as external dangers.

"To give the new system its proper energy, it will be desirable to have it ratified by the authority of the people, and not merely by that of the legislatures.

"I am afraid you will think this project, if not extravagant, absolutely unattainable, and unworthy of being attempted. Conceiving it myself to go no farther than is essential, the objections drawn from this source are to be laid aside. I flatter myself, however, that they may be less formidable on trial than in contemplation. The change in the principle of representation will be relished by a majority of the states, and those too of most influence. The Northern states will be reconciled to it by the *actual* superiority of their populousness; the Southern by their *expected* superiority on this point. This principle established, the repugnance of the large states to part with power will in a great degree subside, and the smaller states must ultimately yield to the predominant will. It is also already seen by many, and must by degrees be seen by all, that, unless the Union be organized efficiently on republican principles, innovations of a much more objectionable form may be obtruded, or, in the most favorable event, the partition of the empire into rival and hostile confederacies will ensue."

When it finally came, the proposal to do something about the ineffective Articles of Confederation was not the direct result of public demand or firm leadership. It was arrived at through the back door, so to speak, and indirectly stemmed from one of the many violations of the Articles by two states. Article VI provided that: "No two or more states shall enter into any treaty, confederation or alliance between them, without the consent of the United States in Congress assembled."

In March, 1785, commissioners from Virginia and Maryland—including Madison and Mason from the former and Samuel Chase from the latter—met at Alexandria and soon moved to Mount Vernon. George Washington was their host but took no part in their discussions for an agreement concerning the jurisdiction of their joint boundary, the Potomac River, and a plan for sharing the expense for marking a channel in Chesapeake Bay. There was also some talk about a canal linking the headwaters of the Potomac with the Ohio—a pet project of Washington's—and another connecting the Delaware with Chesapeake Bay. These would involve Pennsylvania and Delaware, so when the results of the Mount Vernon conference were submitted to the legislatures, Maryland proposed that these two states be invited to discuss a broader agreement on trade and commerce.

This prompted Virginia, at the suggestion of James Madison, to go a step further and invite all the other states to send commissioners to a general trade convention to be held at Annapolis in September, 1786. In this Congress was deliberately ignored. Madison noted, "From the legislative journals of Virginia it appears that a vote to apply for the sanction of Congress was followed by a vote against a communication of the compact to Congress." It seems evident that at least some of the individuals were anxious to avoid publicity.

Nine states appointed delegates to meet at Annapolis. Those from four did not arrive in time to participate. Only New York, New Jersey, Delaware, Virginia, and Pennsylvania were represented. The twelve delegates from these states could accomplish nothing on a national basis, so they adjourned after Alexander Hamilton had drafted an address to the state legislatures. This stated that the delegates unanimously agreed "That there are important defects in the system of federal government . . . of a nature so serious as, in the view of your Commissioners, to render the situation of the United States delicate and critical." The address continued to propose, "the appointment of Commissioners, to meet in Philadelphia on the second Monday in May next, to take into consideration the situation of the United States, to devise such further provisions as shall appear to them necessary to render the constitution of the federal government adequate to the exigencies of the union."

It is interesting that all of the steps leading to the Constitutional Convention were afterthoughts. Two states met to discuss the navigation of a common water boundary. Tacked on to their report was a suggestion that other states might join in a discussion of trade. New Jersey then instructed her delegates to Annapolis "to consider how far a uniform system in their commercial regulations *and other important matters* might be necessary to the common interest and permanent harmony of the several states. These "other important matters" became the subject of Hamilton's address to the state legislatures.

After the Annapolis convention the French chargé d'affaires, Louis Otto, addressed a confidential report to the Comte de Vergennes, his superior in Paris. Although the letter reflects the Gallic cynicism and guile of its writer, this analysis of a shrewd outside observer is pertinent because it contained some grains of truth. Monsieur Otto wrote:

"Although there are no nobles in America, there is a class of men denominated 'gentlemen,' who, by reason of their wealth, their talents, their education, their families, or the offices they hold, aspire to a pre-eminence which the people refuse to grant them; and, although many of these men have betrayed the interests of their order to gain popularity, there reigns among them a connection so much the more intimate as they almost all of them dread the efforts of the people to despoil them of their possessions, and, moreover, they are creditors, and therefore interested in strengthening the government, and watching over the execution of the laws.

"These men generally pay very heavy taxes, while the small proprietors escape the vigilance of the collectors. The majority of them being merchants, it is for their interest to establish the credit of the United States in Europe on a solid foundation by the exact payment of debts, and to grant to Congress powers extensive enough to compel the people to contribute for this purpose. The attempt, my lord, has been vain, by pamphlets and other publications, to spread notions of justice and integrity, and to deprive the people of a freedom which they have so misused. By proposing a new organization of the federal government all minds would have been revolted; circumstances ruinous to the commerce of America have happily arisen to furnish the reformers with a pretext for introducing innovations.

"They represented to the people that the American name had become opprobrious among all nations of Europe; that the flag of the United States was everywhere exposed to insults and annoyance; the husbandman, no longer able to export his produce freely, would soon be reduced to want; it was high time to retaliate, and to convince foreign powers that the United States would not with impunity suffer such a violation of the freedom of trade, but that strong measures could be taken only with the consent of the thirteen states, and that Congress, not having the necessary powers, it was essential to form a general assembly instructed to present to Congress the plan for its adoption, and to point out the means of carrying it into execution.

"The people, generally discontented with the obstacles in the way of commerce, and scarcely suspecting the secret motives of their opponents, ardently embraced this measure, and appointed commissioners, who were to assemble at Annapolis in the beginning of September.

"The authors of this proposition had no hope, nor even desire, to see the success of this assembly of commissioners, which was only intended to prepare a question much more important than that of commerce. The measures were so well taken that at the end of September no more than five states were represented at Annapolis, and the commissioners from the northern states tarried several days at New York in order to retard their arrival.

"The states which assembled, after having waited nearly three weeks, separated under the pretext that they were

not in sufficient numbers to enter on business, and, to jus-
tify this dissolution, they addressed to the different legislatures and to Congress a report, the translation of which I
have the honor to enclose to you."

Virginia took immediate action on the Annapolis report
and appointed delegates to attend the proposed meeting at
Philadelphia. New Jersey quickly followed, and within a
few weeks Pennsylvania, North Carolina, and Delaware
made similar appointments. Congress failed to take any
action for five months. Then when it became evident that
the proposed convention had sufficient support to assure its
existence and that the states might ignore their national
legislature even in a matter that effected its very existence,
Congress approved a proposal made by New York.

"Whereas there is provision in the Articles of Confederation and perpetual Union, for making alterations
therein, ... And whereas experience hath evinced, that
there are defects in the present Confederation, as a means
to remedy which, several of the states . . . have suggested a convention for the purposes expressed in the following Resolution. . . .

"Resolved, That in the opinion of Congress, it is expedient, that on the second Monday in May next, a Convention of Delegates, who shall have been appointed by the
several States, be held at Philadelphia, for the sole and
express purpose of revising the Articles of Confederation,
and reporting to Congress and the several Legislatures,
such alterations and provisions therein, as, shall when
agreed to in Congress, and confirmed by the States, render
the federal Constitution adequate to the exigencies of
Government, and the preservation of the Union."

Six other states quickly appointed delegates. New Hampshire was willing but did not have the money to pay travel expenses. When John Langdon offered to foot the bill personally, the twelfth state concurred. Rhode Island, whose legislature was controlled by farmers with a deep affection for paper money, boycotted the meeting.

The Gentlemen at Philadelphia

On Sunday, May 13, 1787, George Washington wrote in his diary: "At Gray's Ferry the city light horse, commanded by Colonel Miles, met me and escorted me in by the artillery officers who stood arranged and saluted as I passed. . . . Being . . . warmly and kindly pressed by Mr. and Mrs. Robert Morris to lodge with them I did so. . . . Waited on the President, Doctor Franklin, as soon as I got to town. On my arrival the bells were chimed."

Unfortunately, history does not record what the two great Americans discussed as they sat in Franklin's garden in Philadelphia on that spring day. This was but their third meeting during the many years that both had spent in their country's service. They had first met thirty-two years before, when Franklin visited Braddock's headquarters, to which the young Washington was attached as an aide. During the early months of the Revolution Franklin had visited Washington's headquarters at Cambridge to lend the new Commander-in-Chief moral support. Perhaps as they sat in the May sunshine they talked of old times.

More likely, though, they discussed the approaching convention, to which both were rather doubting delegates. But Franklin was not as pessimistic as some about the Articles of Confederation, and he hoped that good would come from the meeting. "Indeed," he wrote Jefferson, "if it does not do good it must do harm, as it will show that we have not wisdom enough among us to govern ourselves and will strengthen the opinion of some political writers that popular governments cannot long support themselves."

Washington had at first refused to serve as a delegate, pleading that he had announced his retirement at the end of the war. He finally agreed to go, reluctantly, "as my friends, with a degree of solicitude which is unusual, seem to wish my attendance." The true reason for his reluctance was his fear of the effect of failure on his reputation, which he expressed in a letter to Virginia's governor. "I very much fear that all of the states will not appear in convention, and that some of them will come fettered so as to impede, rather than accelerate, the great object of their convening which, under the peculiar circumstances of my case, would place me in a more disagreeable situation than any other member would stand in. As I have yielded however to what appeared to be the earnest wishes of my friends, I will hope for the best." The great Virginian was also concerned about the caliber and character of the men who would be delegates.

In this his fears were, in the main, groundless. Despite the cynical Monsieur Otto's assumption that the proposal to remodel the central government was a plot to "put something over" on the people by a moneyed class, most of the fifty-five delegates who attended the convention were sincere, dedicated men. There were a few—a very few—who were self-seeking politicians. There were others, like Alexander Hamilton, who wanted a government in which an aristocracy based on wealth, social position, and education would rule the masses. But the great majority of the delegates came to Philadelphia for the purpose expressed by James Wilson of Pennsylvania. "After the lapse of six thousand years since the creation of the world America now presents the first instance of a people assembled to weigh deliberately and calmly and to decide leisurely and peaceably upon the form of government by which they will bind themselves and their posterity." The delegates may not have been entitled to Thomas Jefferson's appellation "an assembly of demigods," but the group included some of the wisest and best-informed men in the country. They approached their work with a seriousness typified by Gouverneur Morris, who declared, "The whole human race will be affected by the proceedings of this convention." James Madison added that they were meeting "now to decide forever the fate of Republican government."

The French chargé was right about one thing: most of the delegates did represent a gentry who were the ruling class. He was wrong when he said that they "aspired to a pre-eminence which the people refused to grant them." The bulk of the American people in that day took it for granted that their political destinies would be guided by a relatively small group of men whose social position, wealth, or learning entitled them to positions of leadership. Indeed, there was a belief, among the men themselves and the people in general, that such qualifications carried an obligation to public service. And in most states only men of property could hold high public office. In South Carolina the possession of two hundred pounds free of debt was a requirement for a state senator. One hundred pounds was sufficient in New York and New Jersey. In some states there were religious qualifications to be met.

In general, it was a fact of democracy in that day that only men of wealth or position were qualified for political positions of leadership. Although bills of rights in the state constitutions stated that government rested on the consent of the governed, in most of these constitutions it was carefully specified that this consent should be limited to property owners. In Massachusetts every voter had to have an estate of sixty pounds, in New Jersey fifty pounds, in Delaware and Connecticut forty pounds, in Maryland thirty pounds. As an alternative, in these and other colonies, ownership of a certain amount of land was a requirement. As a result, less than one fifth of the adult, white, free, male population could vote. Since women, Negroes, and Indians were excluded from the franchise, the voters of that day represented about 5 per cent of those who would now be qualified to vote.

When the Philadelphia newspapers printed "an exact list of the members of the convention," the list was headed by those who had gained the title "His Excellency" or "The Honorable Governor." This was followed by "Honorable Delegates to Congress," and the list ended with the "following respectable Characters." Most of the delegates were in the first two classifications.

Many of the fifty-five men who at one time or another attended the convention were surprisingly young to occupy positions of national leadership; the average age was forty-two. Four were in their twenties. The oldest member, Benjamin Franklin, eighty-one, could have been the father of all but two or three of the others and the grandfather of almost three quarters of them. Although about one sixth were foreign-born, most had served with distinction in the Revolution, and forty-one had served in Congress.

Although the two best-known delegates, Franklin and Washington, had little formal schooling, twenty-nine of the others were college graduates; Harvard, Yale, Princeton, Columbia, William and Mary, Oxford, and the Universities of Glasgow and Edinburgh were represented. Over thirty had legal training, fourteen had served as state judges or attorneys, and seven were governors or ex-governors. There were four professors or college presidents, two doctors, five businessmen, and four who are best described as "gentlemen of fortune." Seven had signed the Declaration of Independence, and one, John Dickinson, had been there but refused to sign.

William Pierce, a delegate from Georgia, wrote character vignettes of all but two of his confreres, which are invaluable as an evaluation of the framers of the Constitution by a contemporary. Himself a man of humor and good sense, Pierce seems to have had a knack for character analysis. Except that he was sometimes lenient of faults and weaknesses—he did not mention, for instance, that one delegate was an incipient alcoholic—historians generally can find little fault with the pictures he drew of the men with whom he sweated out the summer of 1787. Quotation marks in the paragraphs that follow indicate material from Pierce's document.

The northernmost state, New Hampshire, sent a two-man delegation headed by John Langdon, the man who was paying the bill. Pierce describes Langdon as "a man of considerable fortune, [who] possesses a liberal mind and a good plain understanding." He was a wealthy businessman of forty-six, ex-governor of the state, and speaker of the house. His fellow delegate, Nicholas Gilman, was thirty-two and "modest, genteel and sensible. There is nothing brilliant or striking in his character, but there is something respectable and worthy in the man." Others considered Gilman as something of a self-seeking politician.

Massachusetts sent two merchants and two lawyers. Elbridge Gerry, aged forty-three, was one of the former, also an ex-congressman and active in state politics. Pierce said that he was "very much of a gentleman in his principles and manners" and "marked for his integrity and perseverance." Since Gerry apparently could not distinguish between what was essential and what was trivial his "perseverance" was at times a nuisance. Nathaniel Gorham, the other businessman, left the chair as president of Congress to attend the convention. At age forty-nine he was "high in reputation and much in the esteem of his countrymen . . . a man of very good sense but not much improved in his education." Rufus King, ex-congressman, aged thirty-two, had a "good classical as well as legal knowledge . . . clear and convincing in his arguments, rapid and irrestible at times in his eloquence, but he is not always equal. . . . But take him *tout en semble,* he may with propriety be ranked among the luminaries of the age." Caleb Strong, forty-two, was "greatly in the esteem of his colleagues." He was one of the few who represented the country people of his state.

The three-man team from Connecticut was by far the best of the northern delegations. William Samuel Johnson, sixty-year-old lawyer and judge and recently elected President of Columbia College, was regarded as one of the most learned men in the country, with a Doctor of Laws from Oxford. Pierce felt that "there is nothing in him which warrants the high reputation that he has for public speaking," but reported that he "engages the hearts of men by the sweetness of his temper."

Roger Sherman at sixty-six "exhibits the oddest shaped character I ever remember to have met with. He is awkward, unmeaning and unaccountably strange in his manner. . . . Yet he deserves infinite praise. If he cannot embellish he can furnish thoughts that are wise and useful. He . . . is extremely artful in accomplishing any particular purpose;—it is remarked that he seldom fails." Another contemporary described this ex-shoemaker, ex-almanac maker, lawyer, and judge more bluntly. "He is as cunning as the Devil, and if you attack him you ought to know him well. . . . If he expects you are trying to take him, you may as well catch an eel by the tail." Oliver Ellsworth was a forty-two-year-old judge of the state supreme court, "a gentleman with a clear, deep and copious understanding . . . always attentive to his duty."

New York's three-man delegation was confusing in its make-up. Alexander Hamilton was such an extreme proponent of a strong federal government that his views and statements were somewhat discounted by moderates. The other two New Yorkers, Robert Yates and John Lansing, fervently opposed the strengthening of the central government and left the convention when it became apparent that they were part of a small minority.

Thirty-year-old Alexander Hamilton was perhaps the smallest man physically and the largest intellectually (always excepting Franklin) who attended the convention. A poor orator, "Colonel Hamilton requires time to think. He inquires into every part of his subject with the searching of philosophy, and when he comes forward he comes charged with highly interesting matter. There is no skimming over the surface of a subject with him; he must sink to the bottom to see what the bottom rests on."

Forty-nine-year-old Robert Yates was a lawyer and judge of the state supreme court, "a man of great legal abilities but not distinguished as an orator." Thirty-two-year-old John Lansing was a lawyer and local politician, mayor of Albany and ex-congressman: "his legal knowledge . . . is not extensive nor is his education a good one."

New Jersey's five-man delegation was headed by the state's governor, William Livingston, "about sixty years old and remarkably healthy." Pierce considered him "a man of first rate talents, but he appears to me rather to indulge in sportiveness of wit than a strength of thinking." Forty-two-year-old David Brearly was chief justice of the state, "a man of good, rather than brilliant parts." William Paterson, "about thirty-four years of age and of a very low stature," was "one of those kind of men whose powers break in upon you and create wonder and astonishment. . . . He is a classic, a lawyer and an orator." He was also an ex-congressman and attorney general of the state. William C. Houston, forty-one, on whom Pierce did not comment, was a lawyer and professor of mathematics at Princeton. Twenty-seven-year-old Jonathan Dayton, the youngest delegate, was a "young gentleman of talents, with ambition to exert them." He also had a nasty temper which was "injurious to him."

Second only to Virginia's delegates in ability and prestige was Pennsylvania's eight-man group. By a special act
of the legislature the state's governor, Benjamin Franklin,
had been added to the delegation after it was appointed.
He was, said Pierce, "Well known to be the greatest phi-
losopher of the present age—the very heavens obey
him. . . . He is no speaker, nor does he seem to let politics engage his attention. He is, however, a most extraordinary man and tells a story in a style more engaging
than anything I ever heard. . . . He possesses an activity
of mind equal to a youth of twenty-five years of age."
Franklin contributed little to the convention other than
the prestige of his presence—and its only memorable anec-
dotes. The mere fact that he and Washington were there
had much to do with getting the Constitution ratified.

In addition to Franklin the Pennsylvania delegation
contained three brilliant men: Robert Morris, Gouverneur Morris, and James Wilson. The first Morris had
been the financial genius of the Revolution and at fifty-
three was "a merchant of great eminence and wealth; an
able financier and a worthy patriot. . . . I am told that
when he speaks in the Assembly of Pennsylvania that he
bears down all before him." Much was expected from him
at the convention because of his financial competence, but,
said Pierce, "he never once spoke on any point."

Gouverneur Morris, then in his thirty-fifth year, was
"bred to the law but . . . disliked the profession and
turned merchant. . . . [He] is one of those geniuses in
whom every species of talents combine to render him conspicuous and flourishing in public debate. . . . But with
all these powers he is fickle and inconstant." Because of his

inconsistency Morris was admired more than he was trusted—and, despite his wooden leg and crippled arm, his morals were suspect. James Wilson, forty-five, was regarded as one of the ablest lawyers in America. "Government seems to have been his peculiar study, all the political institutions of the world he knows in detail." He was a staunch champion of the people, who rebuked his monied confreres' concern for property by saying, "I do not agree that property is the sole or primary concern of government."

The lesser lights from Pennsylvania included forty-three-year-old General Thomas Mifflin, who had regained the popular respect he had lost because of his part in the "cabal" against Washington during the war. George Clymer, forty-eight, was a lawyer and "a respectful man, much esteemed." Thomas FitzSimons "is a merchant of considerable talents." Jared Ingersoll "is a very able attorney . . . well educated in the classics and is a man of very extensive reading."

Little Delaware sent five men to protect her rights, and was the only state to limit the authority of its delegates by instructing them not to approve any alterations that would change "that part of the fifth article of the Confederation . . . which declares that, 'In determining the questions in the United States in Congress assembled each state shall have one vote.' "

Most noted of the Delaware delegation was fifty-five-year-old, timid John Dickinson, a Quaker. Although he had refused to sign the Declaration of Independence, he had regained sufficient esteem to become governor of both Pennsylvania and Delaware, and was highly regarded as the author of the *Farmer's Letters*. He did not impress

Pierce, who said, "with an affected air of wisdom he labors to produce a trifle."

George Read, fifty-four, was "a lawyer and a judge. His legal abilities are said to be very great, but his powers of oratory are fatiguing and tiresome to the last degree." Gunning Bedford, Jr., forty, was a lawyer "warm and impetuous in his temper and precipitate in his judgment." He was also "very corpulent." Richard Bassett, forty-two, was "a religious enthusiast, lately turned Methodist, and serves his country because it is the will of the people that he should do so. He is a man of plain sense and has modesty enough to hold his tongue." Jacob Broom, thirty-five was, like Bassett, one of the "respectable characters" at the end of the list; "a plain good man with some abilities, but nothing to render him conspicuous."

Maryland's five men included Luther Martin, thirty-nine, a politician and attorney general of the state who opposed the establishing of a strong national government throughout the Convention. He had a "good deal of information" but was "so extremely prolix that he never speaks without tiring the patience of all who hear him." Dr. James McHenry, thirty-four, as a surgeon in the Revolution; "a man of specious talents with nothing of genius to improve them." Daniel Carroll and John Francis Mercer, both about thirty, were two "gentlemen of fortune" and "respectable characters" who were becoming politically prominent in their state. Daniel of St. Thomas Jenifer, sixty-four, was also a "gentleman of fortune" who "sits silent in the Senate, and seems to be conscious that he is no politician. From his long continuance in single life no doubt he has made the vow of celibacy. He speaks warmly of the ladies notwithstanding."

Greatest by far of the state delegations in prestige, ability, and dedication, was the seven-man group from Virginia. It was headed by the fifty-five-year-old Washington, of whom Pierce wrote: "Having conducted these states to independence and peace, he now appears to assist in framing a government to make the people happy. Like Gustavus Vasa he may be said to be the deliverer of his country; like Peter the Great he appears as the politician and statesman; and like Cincinnatus he returned to his farm perfectly contented with being only a plain citizen, after enjoying the highest honor of the Confederacy—and now only seeks for the approbation of his countrymen by being virtuous and useful."

Tall, commanding, dignified, Washington was the most conspicuous of the Virginia group. Slight, retiring, thirty-seven-year-old James Madison was the least conspicuous. Few would then have labeled him "The Father of the Constitution," but Pierce had an inkling of his ability when he wrote, "Mr. Madison is a character who has long been in public life; and what is very remarkable every person seems to acknowledge his greatness. He blends together the profound politician with the scholar. In the management of every great question he evidently took the lead in the convention. . . . From a spirit of industry and application which he possesses in a most eminent degree, he always comes forward the best informed man on any point in debate. The affairs of the United States, he perhaps, has the most correct knowledge of, of any man in the union. . . . A gentleman of great modesty—with a remarkably sweet temper."

To back these two luminaries were Edmund Randolph, thirty-four-year-old Governor of Virginia who "came forward with the postulata, or first principles, on which the convention acted and supported them with a force of eloquence and reasoning that did him great honor." A handsome gentleman with polished manners, Randolph was a fine figurehead for his able colleagues.

George Mason, sixty-two, was "one of the best politicians in America," and according to Madison, he possessed "the greatest talents for debate" of any man he had ever seen or heard speak. Mason was an avowed champion of the rights of the people who had written the "Bill of Rights" in the Virginia state constitution, on which Jefferson had undoubtedly leaned in writing the Declaration of Independence.

George Wythe, sixty-one, had been Thomas Jefferson's law professor at William and Mary. "No man is said to understand the history of government better than Mr. Wythe,—nor anyone who understands the fluctuating conditions to which all societies are liable better than he does, yet from his too favorable opinion of men, he is no great politician. He is remarked for his exemplary life and universally esteemed for his good principles."

John Blair, at fifty-five was "one of the most respectable men of Virginia, both on account of his family as well as fortune. He is one of the judges of the Supreme Court in Virginia, and is acknowledged to have a very extensive knowledge of the laws." This unusual delegation was completed by forty-one-year-old Dr. James McClurg, "a learned physician, but having never appeared before in public life his character as a politician is not sufficiently known. He attempted to speak once or twice but with no great success." Dr. McClurg had been appointed when Patrick Henry refused to serve.

Virginia's southern neighbor, North Carolina, sent a rather mediocre delegation after some of her best men refused to serve. Ex-governor Alexander Martin, forty-seven, had been dismissed from the army after the battle of Germantown, because, said Pierce, he proved unfit for the field. The actual charge was cowardice. Nevertheless he was "a man of sense and undoubtedly a good politician." William R. Davis, thirty-one, was "said to have a good classical education, and is a gentleman of considerable literary talents. He was silent in the convention." Richard D. Spaight, twenty-nine, was "a worthy man of some ability and fortune, without possessing a genius to render him brilliant." Dr. Hugo Williamson, fifty-two, had been a preacher and professor of mathematics, and "in his manners there is a strong trait of a gentleman." Another contemporary reported that it was hard to know his character well, and it was even possible that he did not have any. William Blount, thirty-eight, "does not possess any of those talents that make men shine—he is plain, honest and sincere."

South Carolina's four-man delegation was somewhat more able. Ex-governor John Rutledge, forty-eight, was a capable lawyer and great orator who was described—not by Pierce—as "one of the claims to fame of South Carolina," whose "reputation in the first Congress gave him a distinguished rank among the American worthies." Charles Cotesworth Pinckney, forty-one, was an ex-brigadier general, a lawyer, Oxford graduate, and socially prominent figure. "When he spoke he was listened to with respect." His younger cousin, Charles Pinckney, thirty, had a "very great variety of knowledge. Government, law, history and philosophy are his favorite studies. . . . [He] had a spirit of application and industry beyond most men." Pierce Butler, forty-three, was of noble birth and an ex-British officer. He was "a gentleman of fortune and takes top rank among the first in South Carolina."

Georgia's four-man team included William Few, thirty-nine, a self-made lawyer who "possesses a strong natural genius" and who served in Congress "with fidelity to his state and honor to himself." Abraham Baldwin, thirty-three, was a lawyer, ex-tutor at Yale, ex-army chaplain, and later president of the University of Georgia. He was "a gentleman of superiority abilities," with "an accommodating turn of mind which enables him to gain the confidence of men and to understand them." The best Pierce could say about the thirty-two-year-old lawyer William Houstoun was that he was "of amiable and sweet temper and of good and honorable principles." He added, scathingly: "Nature seems to have done more for his corporeal than mental powers. His person is striking but his mind little improved with useful or elegant knowledge." William Pierce, forty-seven, did not delineate his own character, saying he would "leave those who may choose to speculate on it to consider it in any light that their fancy or imagination may depict." Nearly fifty, he was a congressman who had served with distinction in the Revolution.

This group was certainly not "an assembly of demigods," but it did merit more than the faint praise of another contemporary, who wrote: "I do not wish to detract from their merits, but I will venture to affirm that twenty assemblies of equal number might be collected, equally respectable both in point of ability, patriotism and integrity. Some of the characters who compose it I revere; others I consider as of small consequence, and a number are suspected of being great public defaulters." Not twenty assemblies nor two could have been gathered that would have been of equal ability without such men as Franklin, Washington, Madison, and Hamilton. Even without these great luminaries, a convention that contained such men as Wythe and Mason from Virginia, the two Morrises and Wilson from Pennsylvania, Johnson, Sherman, and Ellsworth from Connecticut, Rutledge and the Pinckneys from South Carolina, Dickinson from Delaware, Gerry from Massachusetts, and several others, was certainly a body of far better than average men.

Sixty-five men had been appointed to the Convention; ten never attended. Several who were appointed were second choices, after the preferred men refused to serve. Some who refused to attend agreed with Monsieur Otto's view that this proposed revision of the government was a plan for the rich to get richer at the expense of the liberties of the common people. Patrick Henry was one such. He refused to serve, saying laconically, "I smell a rat." Others, like Washington, realized that the Convention might ruin them politically. Some still believed that their most important civic duty was on the home front in their own states. Five of Maryland's top men turned down appointments because a paper money proposal was under consideration in the state, and they considered it necessary to stay home and fight it.

Many of the fifty-five delegates did not attend the Convention regularly or for its entire length. The average attendance at each session was slightly over thirty. There was a hard core of about twenty who attended regularly and did most of the work.

The Convention was supposed to start on May 14, but

when that day dawned only Pennsylvania and Virginia were represented in Philadelphia. There delegates met and adjourned from day to day while they awaited a quorum. Meanwhile, Gouverneur Morris expressed the opinion of the Pennsylvania delegation that "the large states should unite firmly in refusing to the small states an equal vote, as unreasonable, and as enabling the small states to negative every good system of government." Fortunately, wiser heads among the Virginia delegation refused to accept this principle on the grounds that it might "beget fatal altercations between large and small states." It would have done more than this. Had Morris's proposal been vigorously pushed, the Convention would have ended almost before it started with a walkout by at least some of the small states.

By May 25 nine states had at least one delegate each in Philadelphia, and the Convention held its first business session in a room on the second floor of the Pennsylvania State House. The street outside had been spread with earth to prevent traffic noise from disrupting their deliberations; sentries guarded the door to prevent people from disturbing the assembly.

The first order of business was a motion by Robert Morris, proposing "George Washington, Esquire, late Commander-in-Chief, for President of the Convention." John Rutledge of South Carolina seconded, "expressing his confidence that the choice would be unanimous." It was so voted, and Washington was escorted to the chair by Morris and Rutledge; "from which, in a very emphatic manner, he thanked the Convention for the honor they had conferred upon him; reminded them of the novelty of the scene of business in which he was to act, lamented his want of better qualifications, and claimed the indulgence of the house toward the involuntary errors which his inexperience might occasion."

Because of the reverence in which Washington was universally held, his opinion carried great weight on any national question. He spoke only once to any question; but he did let his stand become known. Gouverneur Morris reported that during the informal discussions before a quorum arrived, there was some talk that half measures would probably meet with public approval more than a thorough reform. To this Washington replied: "It is probable that no plan we propose will be adopted. Perhaps another dreadful conflict is to be sustained. If to please the people we offer what we ourselves disapprove, how can we afterwards defend our work? Let us raise a standard to which the wise and honest can repair. The event is in the hand of God."

James Wilson of Pennsylvania nominated Temple Franklin, Benjamin's grandson, for the post of secretary. Alexander Hamilton nominated Major William Jackson, who had been electioneering for the job in the hope that it would lead to future political preferment. Jackson got five votes to Franklin's two and was appointed secretary. He received only $844 for his four months' work of keeping the Convention journal. When this document was finally published in 1818, edited by John Quincy Adams, it became apparent that Jackson had been overpaid. It contains nothing but a list of the motions offered and a record of the vote by states. Beyond this it gives no inkling about who did what at the convention—or even who was there. Were it not for Madison's personal journal, which was not published until after his death, history would have no rec-

ord of how the United States Constitution came into
being.

This secrecy surrounding the proceedings stemmed from
a motion offered by Pierce Butler of South Carolina on the
second day of the Convention, which proposed that the
house should "Provide . . . against licentious publication
of their proceedings." This was incorporated in the rules
by a provision that "Nothing spoken in the house be
printed, or otherwise published, or communicated without
leave." Although this smacks of star chamber proceedings,
it was a wise provision. Had outsiders known what was
going on in the closed room in Philadelphia during that
summer it is probable that so much pressure would have
been brought on delegates by different groups and factions
that nothing would have been agreed to.

So the work of hammering out a charter of government
unique in history started, and it would continue for five
hours a day, six days a week for almost four months—until
September 17—with but a two-day recess over the Fourth
of July and ten days between July 26 and August 6, when
the Committee on Detail prepared the first draft of what
had been accomplished to that time.

3

The Great Compromise

Labels can be confusing. They can mean different things to different people at different times and in different places. In connection with the Constitution the word *federal* is a case in point. During the controversy over the ratification of the Constitution a Federalist was one who favored the strong central government proposed in that document. During the Constitutional Convention, *federal* meant just the opposite; a Federalist was one who favored a continuation of the Federation, in which state power was supreme. Those who favored a strong central government were called Nationalists.

This is important because the question of whether the country should have a "federal" or a "national" government was the great controversy of the Convention, the reef on which the assembly very nearly foundered. The small states favored a federal government in which they would

have an equal voice with the large states and in which
their sovereignty would be protected. The large states
favored a national government that represented the people
rather than the states. Most of the delegates from the large
states—with some exceptions like Mason and Madison of
Virginia and Wilson of Pennsylvania—were not motivated
in this by their concern for the rights of the individual.
Their position was based upon the fact that their states
had more people and would therefore have more influence
in a government based on population.

The most populous states were Virginia, Pennsylvania,
North Carolina, and Massachusetts, in that order. The
small states that were represented during the early weeks
of the Convention were Connecticut, New Jersey, Delaware, and Maryland. Because their population expansion
was so rapid, South Carolina and Georgia expected to become large states and usually, but not always, voted with
this group. New York was, at that time, of moderate size
and sided with the small states. Rhode Island would never
be represented in the Convention, and the New Hampshire delegation did not arrive until after the most mo-
mentous question was decided.

Much has been said about a supposed division between
the North and the South at the Constitutional Convention, although on the major points no such rift existed. By
the time Madison's journal was published slavery and
North-South economic differences had become paramount,
and great significance was given to any indication of sectional discord in his records of the debates. Actually, Virginia and Massachusetts stood shoulder to shoulder in
Philadelphia. Madison is one of the few men at the Convention who seemed to realize that the North-South con-

flict was of greater potential significance than the big-state–little-state conflict; at least he is the only one who mentioned that "the great danger to our general government is the great southern and northern interests of the continent being opposed to each other."

On many of the most important problems with which the Convention was to wrestle there was surprising unanimity. Most delegates agreed that there must be some kind of a new continental government; that there should be a Congress probably consisting of two houses; that it should have the power to raise money, regulate interstate relations and international commerce, and compel the obedience of the states in matters that were purely federal; that there should be an executive branch of the government; that there should be a federal judiciary. These matters had been the subject of endless discussion for years, and there was general agreement on them, although there would be a good deal of discussion of details. The one point on which there was complete disagreement was the extent to which the states should remain sovereign.

The big states made the first move. While awaiting a quorum the Virginia delegates had drawn up a plan that Randolph presented to the Convention as soon as it was organized, on May 29. Although the first resolution in the Virginia Plan stated that the Articles of Confederation should be "corrected and enlarged," the proposals it contained were so radical, in relation to the Articles, that it actually proposed a new instrument of government. Randolph "candidly confessed that they were not intended for a federal government—he meant a strong *consolidated* union." The Virginia Plan consisted of a preamble outlining the defects of the Articles of Confederation, followed by fifteen resolutions. The most important proposals were:

That the Articles should be "corrected and enlarged" to assure the "common defense, security of liberty, and general welfare."

"The rights of suffrage in the national legislature ought to be proportioned to the quotas of contribution [that is, direct taxation] or to the number of free inhabitants."

"The national legislature ought to consist of two branches."

"The members of the first branch of the national legislature ought to be elected by the people of the several states."

"The members of the second branch . . . ought to be elected by those of the first . . . from persons nominated by the individual legislatures."

"The national legislature ought to be empowered . . . to legislate in all cases where the separate states are incompetent."

Congress should have the right "to negative all laws passed by the several states" that, in its opinion, contravened federal law or treaties.

Congress should have the right to "call forth the force of the Union against any member of the Union" to enforce its authority.

"Resolved, that a national executive be instituted; to be chosen by the national legislature."

"Resolved, that a national judiciary be established to consist of one or more supreme tribunals."

The executive and "a convenient number of the national judiciary" should form a council to "examine every act of the national legislature . . . and that the dissent of the said council shall amount to a rejection," unless the act was again passed by an unspecified greater majority of the legislature.

"Resolved, that provision ought to be made for the admission of states," and the republican government and the territory of such states should be guaranteed by the government of the United States.

"Resolved, that provision ought to be made for the amendment of the Articles of Union whensoever it shall seem necessary."

The proposals of the Convention should be submitted to "assemblies of representatives . . . chosen by the people to consider and decide thereon."

Randolph talked for most of the day to present his plan. In the late afternoon young Charles Pinckney of South Carolina offered an alternate proposal of considerable length that he had himself worked out before coming to Philadelphia. Perhaps it was felt that the young man was being presumptuous in this; in any event his plan was not discussed by the Committee of the Whole, to which both plans were referred. The Committee of the Whole, which met for the next twelve days with Gorham of Massachusetts replacing Washington in the chair, was the entire assembly meeting under conditions that permitted more informal discussion.

The initial consideration of the Committee was Randolph's first resolution, "that the Articles of Confederation ought to be corrected and enlarged." Obviously, the Virginia Plan went far beyond this, and the resolution was changed to read, "that a national government ought to be established consisting of a supreme legislative, executive and judiciary." After brief argument as to the meaning of *supreme* this was passed, with only Connecticut dissenting and New York divided. New Jersey and Maryland were not yet represented, and Delaware went along with the majority.

During the next two days the other small-state delegates and the third New York delegate arrived. The question of a two-house legislature was passed unanimously, with Pennsylvania abstaining out of deference to Franklin, who was known to favor a single house. Then came the question of the basis of representation in the legislature; was it to be proportional to population or by states? Only New York, Delaware, and New Jersey held out for state representation in the lower house. The remaining state delegations approved a resolution that representation was to be "in proportion to the whole number of white and other free citizens and inhabitants of every age, sex and condition . . . and three fifths of all other persons . . . except Indians."

On the question of proportional representation in the Senate the small states presented a united front, but lost by a vote of six to five, to a resolution reading, "The right of suffrage in the second branch . . . ought to be according to the rule established for the first."

The question of how legislators should be elected brought out some opinions that are surprising in the light of today's concept of democracy. Madison wrote: "Mr. Sherman opposes election by the people. . . . The people, he said, immediately should have as little to do as may be about the government." Gerry of Massachusetts said: "The evils we experience flow from an excess of democracy. The people do not want virtue, but are the dupes of pretended patriots." Butler of South Carolina "thought an election of the people an impractical mode." But six states finally carried the proposal that members of the lower house should be elected by the people. It was unanimously agreed that senators should be appointed by state legislatures, a method that continued until the seventeenth amendment, in 1913, provided for popular election of senators.

There was little disagreement as to granting the legislature extensive powers so long as such powers were carefully defined. The right to negative state laws that contravened federal law was agreed to, but the power to negative any state law was voted down. The proposal to use force against a state to compel conformity was discussed briefly, postponed, and never brought up again.

There was great confusion about the proposed executive branch of the government. Should it be one man; a triumvirate with equal powers; one man with a council? How should it be chosen? How long should it serve? What powers and duties should it have? These matters were all explored in depth. On only one point was there unanimity: the people were not qualified to elect a chief magistrate. Only Wilson suggested that they should, and he prefaced his proposal with an apology, saying that he was "almost unwilling to declare the mode which he wished to take place, being apprehensive that it might appear chimerical." His proposal for electors chosen by popular vote in districts was overwhelmingly defeated.

After much more or less aimless conversation, in which fears were repeatedly expressed that the chief executive might turn into a monarch, the committee approved the proposal in the Virginia Plan: a single executive chosen by the legislature for a term of seven years and not eligible for re-election. He was to have the right to make appointments "in all cases not otherwise provided for," he was to have a veto power subject to overrule by two thirds of the legislature, and he was subject to impeachment.

There was less discussion of a federal judiciary. A supreme court was agreed to whose judges were to be appointed by the legislature. There was some discussion as to the need for inferior federal courts, and the matter was finally settled, as was so much else, by compromise. The legislature was permitted but not required to establish inferior courts.

The remaining elements of the Virginia Plan aroused little debate. They were approved with minor changes in detail. On June 13, the Committee of the Whole reported out to the Convention—which was, of course, the same body with different rules of procedure—an amended Virginia Plan that now contained nineteen resolutions and that, on the all-important question of proportional representation, was a clear-cut victory for the big states.

During the debate in Committee the leadership on both sides became well established. Madison and Wilson were the strongest advocates of a national government, supported by King and Gerry of Massachusetts, Randolph and Mason of Virginia, the Pinckneys of South Carolina, and Gouverneur Morris of Pennsylvania. A federal government in which the states would retain more control was staunchly supported by Sherman and Ellsworth of Connecticut and Paterson of New Jersey, with assistance from Johnson of Connecticut, Luther Martin of Maryland, Lansing and Yates of New York, Dickinson and Bedford of Delaware, and Brearly of New Jersey. Alexander Hamilton had, as yet, said little; so had Franklin. Washington had said nothing. But their votes indicated that the two most important members of the Convention favored a national government—Washington strongly and Franklin mildly.

On June 4 the small states struck back when Paterson of New Jersey requested permission to present an alternate plan. The New Jersey Plan, which was referred to the Committee of the Whole, contained nine resolutions. It proposed that the Articles of Confederation be retained and amended to give Congress power to raise revenue and enforce its acts on the states. It proposed an executive, presumably plural, to be elected by Congress but without veto power. The other variations from the Virginia Plan were of little consequence.

The New Jersey Plan left the Congress as it was under the Articles—one house with each state having one vote. Under this plan the federal legislature would be an agency of the states; under the Virginia Plan it was the national legislative organ of the people.

The two plans were debated in committee for three days, during which the small-state advocates based their case on the fact that the Convention had been called to amend the Articles of Confederation, not to create a new government. Also, they claimed that their plan was much more likely to receive approval from the country at large. The big-state answer to this was that, although the delegates had the power to conclude nothing, they had a right to propose anything; and they believed that the soundest proposal was for a national government.

During this debate Alexander Hamilton made his only speech at the Convention in which he presented opinions that differed radically from both plans. He advocated a strongly centralized government similar to the British government, which, he said, "was the best in the world." For the Senate he suggested that "we copy the House of Lords in all respects." (Until the Reform Act of 1832 the House of Lords had great influence in the British government.) Senators and the President were to serve for life or "during good behavior." The executive was to have an absolute veto, and the governors of the several states were to be appointed by the central government and have veto powers over the acts of state legislatures.

Later, Hamilton was accused of having proposed a monarchy—which he indignantly denied. Although he did not propose the titles and trappings of royalty, his Senate would have been very similar in purpose to a House of Lords, and his President would have served under the same conditions and have generally the same powers as England's king. The Committee listened to Hamilton's plan and then went on with its business. Johnson said, "The gentleman from New York . . . has been praised by everybody, he has been supported by none." Hamilton left the Convention a few days later. His ideas were too radical, and he was constantly outvoted by his two New York colleagues. He returned for brief visits later and to sign the finished Constitution.

It is possible that had the New Jersey Plan been submitted at the opening of the Convention it would have been accepted as a basis for a beginning, because it represented what most of the delegates believed they had come to Philadelphia to do. But two weeks of discussion had converted the majority of them to the acceptance of what they would originally have considered as radical ideas. When, on June 19, they voted for a choice of the two plans, the Virginia proposal won, seven to four, Connecticut voting with the big states.

The Convention now started to give more detailed consideration to the individual resolutions of the Virginia Plan. For eight days all went well. The big-state men were conciliatory on minor points. They agreed to delete the word *national* as applied to the government. There was a compromise on the term of office in the lower house, reducing it from three years to two. The term of senators was fixed at six years. Other details were agreed to in this lull before the storm. Then, on June 27 Rutledge of South Carolina proposed that the Convention proceed at once to the resolutions involving "the most fundamental points, the rules of suffrage in the two branches."

During the next week it seemed, on several occasions, that the Convention was on the point of breaking up. Gouverneur Morris afterward said, "the fate of America was suspended by a hair." To this time the expressions of opinion had been reasoned and polite. Now they became emotional and acrimonious on a motion by Connecticut that each state should have a single vote in the Senate. With, according to King of Massachusetts, "a vehemence unprecedented in that house," Bedford of Delaware proclaimed: "The large states dare not dissolve the convention. If they do the small ones will find some foreign ally, of more honor and good faith, who will take them by the hand and do them justice." In short, the small states would return to Great Britain.

Bedford's colleague Dickinson snarled at Madison: "You see the consequences of pushing things too far. Some of the members from the small states wish for two branches in the general legislature and are friends to a good national government; but we would sooner submit to foreign power than submit to be deprived, in both branches of the legislature, of an equal suffrage, and thereby be thrown under the domination of the larger states."

"I will never accede to a plan," bawled Martin of Maryland, "that will introduce an inequality and lay ten states at the mercy of Virginia, Massachusetts, and Pennsylvania." Said Lansing, "New York would never have concurred in sending deputies to the Convention if she had supposed the deliberations were to turn on a consolidation of the states and a national government." "New Jersey," said Paterson, "will never confederate on the plan before the committee. She will be swallowed up. I had rather submit to a monarch, a despot, than to such a fate."

Some of the big-state men were equally outspoken. "If the small states," said Wilson, "will not confederate on this plan, Pennsylvania will not confederate on any other. If New Jersey will not part with her sovereignty it is vain to talk of government." When Ellsworth of Connecticut intimated that, if the convention went to pieces, New York and New England would join hands and become an independent nation, Wilson replied: "If the deplored event happen, it will neither stagger my sentiments or my duty. If the minority of the people of America refuse to coalesce with the majority on just and proper principles, if a separation must take place, it could never be on better grounds." Gouverneur Morris topped the debate—or climaxed the battle—by shouting: "This country must be united. If persuasion does not unite, the sword will."

On all of this Madison mildly commented, "Indeed the eagerness displayed by the members opposed to a national government began now to produce serious anxieties for the result of the Convention."

During this turmoil Benjamin Franklin, the freethinker, endeavored to pour oil on the troubled waters by a motion that might have been more readily expected from Richard Bassett, the devout Methodist, or ex-preachers Williamson or Baldwin. Too ill to rise and speak, he wrote out his proposal for his colleague to read:

"In this situation of this assembly, groping, as it were, in the dark, to find political truth, and scarce able to distin-

James Madison, father of the Constitution

The State House in Philadelphia where the Constitutional Convention was held

Gouverneur Morris who actually wrote the Constitution

George Washington, who lent his prestige as President to the Constitutional Convention. The "Lansdowne Portrait" by Gilbert Stuart.

Benjamin Franklin, whose distinguished presence at the Convention helped immeasurably to bring about the ratification of the Constitution. Portrait by Charles Willson Peale.

John Jay who contributed articles to *The Federalist* which helped
to bring about ratification of the Constitution

Alexander Hamilton, whose articles in *The Federalist* helped the ratification of the Constitution

The first page of the original draft of the Constitution

guish it when presented to us, how is it happened, sir, that we have not hitherto once thought of humbly applying to the Father of Lights to illuminate our understandings? In the beginning of the contest with Britain, when we were sensible of danger, we had daily prayers in this room for the Divine protection. Our prayers, sir, were heard—and they were graciously answered. . . . Have we forgotten that powerful Friend? or do we imagine we no longer need Its assistance? I have lived, sir, a long time, and the longer I live the more convincing proofs I see of this truth, that God governs in the affairs of men. And if a sparrow cannot fall to the ground without His notice, is it probable that an empire can rise without His aid? We have been assured, sir, in the sacred writings that 'except the Lord build the house, they labor in vain that build it.' I firmly believe this, and I also believe that without His concurring aid we shall succeed in this political building no better than the builders of Babel; we shall be divided by our little, partial, local interests, our projects will be confounded, and we ourselves shall become a reproach and a byword down to future ages. And, what is worse, mankind may hereafter, from this unfortunate instance, despair of establishing government by human wisdom, and leave it to chance, war, and conquest.

"I therefore beg leave to move—

"That henceforth prayers, imploring the assistance of Heaven and its blessing on our deliberations, be held in this assembly every morning before we proceed to business; and that one or more of the clergy of this city be requested to officiate in that service."

The manuscript of this motion is still extant, with a note in the margin in Franklin's hand, "The Convention, ex-

cept for three or four persons, thought prayers unnecessary." There is a tradition that Hamilton remarked that
the Convention did not need "foreign aid," and Williamson said that "the convention had no funds." The true
reason for ignoring Franklin's proposal was undoubtedly
the fear that sending out for a clergyman might give the
impression that the Convention was ready for the last
rites.

A couple of days later Franklin proposed compromise.
"The diversity of opinion," he said, "turns on two points.
If a proportional representation takes place, the small
states contend that their liberties will be in danger. If an
equality of votes is to be put in its place, the large states say
that their money will be in danger. When a broad table is
to be made, and the edges of the planks do not fit, the
artist takes a little from both and makes a good joint. In
like manner both sides must part with some of their demands, in order that they may join in some accommodating proposition."

The vote on the motion that each state have equal voice
in the upper house represented the first break in the big-
state ranks. Baldwin of Georgia voted "aye," creating a five-
to-five tie by dividing the vote of that state. It is thought
that Baldwin's defection was not based on a change in his
opinions but on a conviction that the small states would
withdraw if this motion was lost. Also, he was a former
Connecticut man and may have had some allegiance to the
northern state.

This created a stalemate in the Convention. After a few
desultory suggestions the older Pinckney proposed that a
committee consisting of one delegate from each state be
elected by ballot to try to reach a compromise. Madison

and Wilson fought this proposal vehemently but lost. The result of the election of committeemen indicated that the small states had won their point even before the committee met. Gerry and Ellsworth were the only strong big-state men included. Baldwin, who had already voted with the small states, was selected from Georgia, and Franklin, who had already proposed compromise, represented Pennsylvania.

This sudden seeming capitulation on the part of the big states indicates that the matter may have been decided in a "smoke-filled room" rather than on the floor of the Convention; or, since *smoke-filled room* has an unpleasant connotation, the procedure might be compared to today's Senate cloakroom, where many agreements are made. Several of the delegates lived together in a "hall" of the Indian Queen Tavern on Fourth Street. There are numerous references to informal, off-the-record discussions during the evenings, here and at social affairs most delegates attended. It is very likely that some agreements between individual members were reached in these discussions that do not appear in the debates.

Since Madison was not on the committee, there is no record of their deliberations. Yates recorded that Franklin made the motion that "after some modification was agreed to, and made the basis of the report of the committee." This report recommended two propositions, "on condition that both be generally adopted." Their substance was this: (1) That the first branch of the legislature (the House of Representatives) should have one representative for each 40,000 inhabitants, counting three fifths of the slaves, and that money bills should originate in the lower house and not be subject to amendment by the upper house;

(2) that in the second branch (the Senate) each state should have an equal vote.

Initial debate on the report was somewhat bitter, with Madison, Wilson, and Gouverneur Morris speaking emphatically against it. But it was obvious that the Convention as a whole was in a mood for compromise. A committee was appointed to advise on exactly how many members should be in the lower house. While they deliberated, some alternative suggestions were made on minor points. One practical addition to the proposal was a decision that "a census be taken within six years . . . and once within the term of every ten years afterwards." The first such census was taken in 1790.

There is a widespread misconception that the so-called three-fifths rule for counting slaves was an important part of the great compromise. This idea developed when, after Madison's journal was published, writers endeavored to show that there had been a North-South conflict during the Convention. The idea of counting three fifths of the slaves was first incorporated in the proposed revenue amendment to the Articles of Confederation in 1783; it was an amendment to the Virginia Plan and contained in the New Jersey Plan. It was no part of the compromise. Rufus King later said that "this rule . . . was adopted because it was the language of all America." During the debate on the compromise South Carolina and Georgia hopefully proposed that slaves be counted equally with whites, but only Delaware supported them on this.

When the Committee on Representation reported, they at first recommended a total of fifty-six members of the lower house. This was revised to sixty-five—a figure that was more or less a guess, because there had been no census, and one that probably short-changed the four big states, whose population may have entitled them to more than the thirty-one seats they were allotted.

On July 16 the compromise was adopted, with Connecticut, Delaware, New Jersey, Maryland, and North Carolina voting for it, and Pennsylvania, Virginia, South Carolina, and Georgia against. Massachusetts was divided, and New York was not represented; Yates and Lansing had gone home in disgust when it became apparent that some form of reasonably strong central government would be recommended by the Convention. The great compromise, the essence of which was equal state representation in the upper house, was the most important single event of the Constitutional Convention, for without it the Convention would not have produced the Constitution.

Oceans of ink have been spread in an effort to allocate the credit for the great compromise, and several of the delegates to the Convention, and their biographers, later advanced claims. It has frequently been called the "Connecticut Compromise," because Johnson of that state brought the subject up and the motion "in the second . . . each should have an equal vote" was made by Connecticut's Ellsworth. But Ellsworth's motion would have been lost had not Baldwin crossed the line and voted for it. The subject had been a matter of general concern since the opening of the Convention, and no individual or state delegation deserves special credit. In the final analysis it was Benjamin Franklin who advanced the actual proposal in committee. Characteristically, Franklin never claimed any credit.

The First Draft

For ten days after the compromise was adopted all was sweetness and light in the City of Brotherly Love—or almost all. Some of the big-state men did not immediately accept defeat graciously and asked for an adjournment until the next day to plan strategy. At a caucus the next morning most were inclined to yield to the will of the Convention, and Madison wrote that the smaller states were probably now satisfied "that they had nothing to apprehend from a union of the larger in any plan whatever against the equality of votes in the second branch." An item appeared in the local press two days after the compromise that may have been a deliberate "leak" from within the Hall: "So great is the unanimity, we hear, that prevails in the Convention, upon all great federal subjects, that it had been proposed to call the room in which they assemble Unanimity Hall."

Although it is not true that there was perfect unanimity, there was, after the great compromise, a new spirit in the Convention and a greater tendency on the part of the delegates to work things out together rather than combat each other in opposing factions. For the balance of the meeting the big-state–small-state line-up had much less influence. Delegates were motivated primarily by their personal views. For instance, on the next important question, Madison was opposed by fellow Virginians Mason and Randolph, and King of Massachusetts disagreed with his colleague Gerry.

This had to do with how the chief executive should be elected. It must be borne in mind that the framers of the Constitution did not visualize the peculiar balance we have today, when the executive department of the government is so prominent and powerful. To them the heart of the government was the legislature; all else was supplementary. Three quarters of the first draft of the Constitution was devoted to the Congress. The executive, the judiciary, the admission of new states, amendments, ratification, oaths of office, and all other matters were dealt with in the final quarter.

Alexander Hamilton wrote, "In republican governments, the legislative authority necessarily predominates"; and Hamilton was the staunchest supporter of a strong executive. He added: "In forming a government which is to be administered by men over men, the great difficulty lies in this—you must first enable the government to control the governed and, in the next place, oblige it to control itself. A dependence on the people is, no doubt, a primary control on the government; but experience has taught mankind the necessity of auxiliary precautions."

One of these "auxiliary precautions" was the division of the legislature into two houses. Another was to be an executive with limited veto power.

But how this executive should be chosen and what his term should be were matters on which there was a wide divergence of opinion. Wilson noted, with apparent satisfaction, "that the idea was gaining ground of an election mediately or immediately by the people." This was, to an extent, wishful thinking on Wilson's part. Although it is true that Gouverneur Morris, King, Paterson, and Dickinson now supported the view that had previously been held only by Wilson and Madison, they were a small minority. The over-all opinion of the Convention was voiced by Mason when he said: "It would be as unnatural to refer the choice of a proper character for chief magistrate to the people, as it would to refer a trial of colors to a blind man. The extent of the country renders it impossible that the people can have the requisite capacity to judge the respective pretentions of the candidates."

Another objection to popular vote was that people would always vote for a man from their own state, and this would give the most populous states an advantage. To get around this it was suggested that everybody should vote for two candidates, only one of whom could be from his own state. Another proposal was that each state should name one man, and the legislature should choose from these thirteen nominees. At one point the Convention passed a motion that the state legislatures should choose electors; one from each of the four smallest states, three from each of the three largest, and two from each of the others. After thinking it over for two days, the assembly reversed itself on the grounds that it would be too expensive for the electors to gather for the single purpose of choosing an executive, and those from the more distant states might not come.

The discussion on the length of term for the President was equally muddled. Everything from four years to "during good behavior" was proposed. If the executive was to be selected by the legislature, he obviously should not be eligible for re-election, otherwise he would be the creature of the legislature. Therefore he should have a long single term, perhaps seven years. If he were selected independently of the legislature, he should have a short term and be eligible for a second term as an incentive to do his work well.

After discussing this subject for several days Gerry said, "We seem to be entirely at a loss." Madison added, "There are objections against every mode that has been, or perhaps can be, proposed." They finally gave up and left the matter as it was in the recommendation of the Committee of the Whole; election by the national legislature for a single seven-year term. The only things that were definitely decided at this point were that the President have limited veto power and be subject to impeachment.

The subject of the judiciary was less troublesome. It was agreed that the supreme federal court should have jurisdiction in "all cases arising under the national laws and to such other questions as may involve the national peace and harmony." As with the President, the method of selecting the Supreme Court judges was the principal point of dispute. Madison led a fight to have them appointed by the President instead of the Senate but was voted down; as was his next proposal, for executive appointment with the "advice and consent of the second branch." The small states were adamant about keeping these appointments exclusively in the Senate, where they had equal representation.

A revival of the proposal to join the judiciary with the executive in the veto power was voted down, and this led to a renewed consideration of the right of Congress to negative state laws. This was taken away on the grounds that the judiciary would have such a right. In this connection a resolution was adopted "that the legislative acts of the United States . . . shall be the supreme law of the separate states . . . and that the judiciaries of the several states shall be bound by their decisions, anything in the respective laws of the individual states to the contrary notwithstanding." It is ironic that this proposal was made by Luther Martin, outstanding foe of a powerful national government. It has developed into one of the most important articles in the Constitution to strengthen the central government.

In line with the growing sentiment to permit the people to have some voice in the government—although not to the extent of selecting a President or senators—ratification of the Constitution by assemblies selected by the people, instead of the state legislatures, was approved. Madison again led the fight for this, saying that he "considered the difference between a system founded on the legislatures only and one founded on the people to be the true difference between a league or treaty and a Constitution."

The final item of interest at this point was the question of the number of senators and how they should vote. Many delegates interpreted the great compromise to mean that each state should have but one vote in the upper house, as in the old Congress. However, the main point was equal representation, and there was little opposition to a proposal for two senators from each state who would vote as individuals.

The fifteen resolutions of the original Virginia Plan had now been increased to twenty-three. With the exception of the provisions of the great compromise, these were all general in nature. The Convention had now reached the point where what they would propose should be made specific. They therefore appointed a five-man Committee of Detail to draw up a first draft; Rutledge of South Carolina, chairman, Randolph of Virginia, Gorham of Massachusetts, Ellsworth of Connecticut, and Wilson of Pennsylvania. Almost as an afterthought, the Convention referred the New Jersey Plan and Pinckney's plan to the Committee. As the Convention was about to adjourn for ten days to let the committee do its work, the two-man delegation from New Hampshire finally arrived.

The work that the Committee of Detail did between July 26 and August 6 is one of the most unsung accomplishments of American history. The Declaration of Independence was a much shorter and less complex document, yet it took the committee that composed it seventeen days to prepare the draft they submitted to Congress.

There are no records of the sessions of the Committee of Detail, but there are documents extant from which its progress can be traced. The first draft was apparently written by Randolph. The manuscript of this has extensive changes, some in Randolph's hand and others in the handwriting of Rutledge. At least the latter were surely the result of Committee discussion, noted by the chairman. The next stage of which there is a record is a draft in the hand of James Wilson, incorporating portions of the revised Randolph draft and excerpts from the New Jersey and Pinckney plans. This was a fairly advanced stage of the work; the changes, again in Rutledge's hand, all have to do with phrasing.

This revised document was printed on seven folio pages with wide margins for making notes. It now contained a preamble and twenty-three articles divided into forty-three sections. The first two articles were introductory; the next seven dealt with Congress; two single short articles covered the executive and judiciary; two placed restrictions upon the states, and three listed state privileges; and the final seven were devoted to the admission of new states, the guarantee of their governments, amendments, oaths of office, ratification, and the inauguration of the new government.

The result of the work of the Committee was a detailed development of the resolutions adopted by the Convention with some minor modifications and major additions. It added the provision that criminal trials in federal courts should be by jury; that the appointment of ambassadors and the making of treaties should be confined to the Senate; that new states should be "admitted on the same terms with the original states"; that the protection of a state "against domestic violence" should be only in cases where such a request was made by the state legislatures.

A thorny minor problem was the payment of salaries to members of the government. Some delegates, particularly Franklin, were opposed to the senior government officers being paid *any* salaries. This was in line with the then generally accepted concept that the country's rulers should come from a wealthy upper class. One of Franklin's few written speeches was devoted to this, and in it he said: "There are two passions which have a powerful influence in the affairs of men. These are ambition and avarice: the love of power and the love of money. Separately, each of these has great force in prompting men to action; but when united in view of the same object, they have in many minds the most violent effects. Place before the eyes of such men a post of honor, that shall at the same time be a place of profit, and they shall move heaven and earth to obtain it." He continued to say that such an incentive would bring into government "men of strong passion and indefatigable activity in their selfish pursuits. These will thrust themselves into your government and be your rulers." Perhaps because most of the delegates would hold posts in the new government, Franklin's motion for no salaries had been voted down. "It was," said Madison, "treated with great respect, but rather for the author of it than from any conviction of its expediency and practicability." The Committee of Detail provided that the members of both houses of Congress be paid by their states and the President by the central government.

The committee made three major additions to the resolutions passed by the Convention—all, it would seem, the work of southerners Rutledge and Randolph. These provided that there be no interference with the slave trade, that no export taxes be laid, and that navigation acts require a two-thirds vote of both houses.

When the Convention reassembled on August 6, they started on a five-week process of considering the Constitution paragraph by paragraph, which was dogged and at times dull, although there were still some important changes to be made, based mainly on the growing receptiveness to a reasonably strong central government. There was much hairsplitting by some delegates and long discussions on matters that now seem to us minor. The militia is a case in point. The relation of the central government to these citizen-soldiers was debated endlessly. Shays' Rebellion was fresh in the minds of the delegates, and at a time when a standing army was generally considered as the arm of a despot, the militia was regarded as of great importance to assure domestic tranquillity and provide for the common defense.

The Convention accepted the Committee's proposal covering the qualifications of voters: that they should be the same as those applied in each state "to the numerous branches of their own legislatures." This decision had the rather surprising consequence that nowhere in the Constitution is *a citizen of the United States* defined. They eliminated a provision that the legislature should have the right to determine property qualifications for members; prohibited congressmen from appointment to any federal office that Congress had created; established twenty-five as the minimum age for the lower house and thirty as the minimum age for the Senate; and agreed to a provision for annual meetings for the legislature. There was some discussion as to when these meetings should take place. Madison held out for May, when travel was easy, but it was pointed out that a summer session would interfere with the other business of the members, who, it was assumed, would probably be "more or less connected with agriculture." They decided on December.

Length of citizenship for Congressmen was increased from three to seven years for the House and from four to nine years for the Senate, to guard against "foreigners" in the legislature. Madison wanted to increase the figure for the number of inhabitants per representative above 40,-

000, because he thought that an inevitable population increase would lead to an unwieldy house. Gorham replied
that the government would not last long enough for that
to happen, saying, "Can it be supposed that this vast country, including the western territory, will 150 years hence
remain one nation?" The matter was compromised by in-
serting the words *not exceeding* before the clause *the rate
of one for every forty thousand.* The only motion to which
Washington spoke was one made and passed in the final
days of the Convention, decreasing this figure to 30,000.

The question of salaries again came up, and the Convention overwhelmingly reversed the Committee and
voted that Congressional salaries be paid out of the national treasury so as to free the national legislature from
state control. The amount of salaries was not fixed, due to
the probability of a change in the value of money. Madison sought to avoid this by proposing that wheat be used as
a standard of value in paying salaries, but the assembly got
around the problem by deciding to allow the legislators to
"fix their own salaries."

There was a rather lengthy debate on the provision that
money bills, which must originate in the lower house,
could not be amended in the Senate. It was twice voted to
eliminate this restriction of the powers of the upper house.
Although the Senate was the small state's favorite branch
of the government, the difference of opinion was not on
state lines. Madison, who disapproved of the restriction,
was opposed by fellow Virginians Washington, Randolph,
and Mason. Franklin, who approved of it, was opposed by
fellow Pennsylvanians Wilson and Morris. Perhaps to explain why the great Washington disagreed with him,
Madison recorded that Washington's vote was not based on

conviction, but that "he gave up his judgment because it was not of very material weight with him and was made an essential point with others who, if disappointed, might be less cordial to other points of real weight."

An important part of the Committee report was the list of powers to be vested in Congress. Although acceptance of a central government was growing, it had not reached the point, by far, of giving such a government a blank check. The delegates considered it their duty to list specifically all of its rights and duties. This list included all the powers held by Congress under the Articles of Confederation, plus several important new ones. The most consequential of these were the right to levy taxes and duties, to regulate interstate commerce, and to call forth the militia "to execute the laws of the Union, enforce treaties, suppress insurrections and repel invasions."

Other new powers granted the Congress included the right to establish uniform bankruptcy and naturalization rules; to define and punish treason; and to provide for the punishment of offenses against the law of nations. An important provision was the right to legislate in all cases where the separate states were incompetent or where the harmony of the Union might be harmed by state legislation. This concluded with the important power to "make all laws that shall be necessary and proper for carrying into execution the foregoing powers, and all other powers vested by this Constitution in the government of the United States or in any department or officer thereof."

There was a rather lengthy discussion as to whether the central government should be permitted to or compelled to assume state debts. Several of the states had certificates outstanding of debts that had been incurred during the

War, many of which had depreciated tremendously and others of which had been bought up by speculators for a few cents on the dollar. Although it was generally agreed, except by those states that had paid off their debts, that the United States should be responsible for the cost of the War, it was obvious that the assumption of state indebtedness at face value would primarily benefit speculators rather than patriots. A committee specially appointed to decide this left it up in the air by ruling that all debts should be "as valid against the United States under this Constitution as under the Confederation." This vagueness was later an important factor in the rift between Hamilton and Jefferson, when both were in Washington's cabinet, from which developed the two-party political system.

Another question that was important then, and was discussed at length, was the basis on which new states should be admitted. The matter of state jealousy was involved here; not between the existing states, but between the original states and any new ones that might be formed out of the western territory. The Committee of Detail had reported that new states should "be admitted on the same terms with the original states." This displeased most of the delegates, particularly Gouverneur Morris, who claimed that he "did not mean to discourage the growth of the western country. . . . He did not wish, however, to throw the power into their hands." The Convention readily agreed to his substitution: "New states may be admitted by the legislature into the Union." This clause was so ambiguous that it could be interpreted in any of a variety of ways. Sixteen years later, in reply to an inquiry about the Louisiana Purchase, Morris himself interpreted it by writing: "Your inquiry . . . is substantially whether the Congress can admit, as a new state, territory which did not belong to the United States when the Constitution was made. In my opinion, they cannot. I have always thought that, when we should acquire Canada and Louisiana, it would be proper to govern them as provinces, and allow them no voice in our councils." Had Morris had his way, Florida, Texas, California, Alaska, Hawaii, and several other states would now be the "provinces."

The Convention next laid some limitations on the powers of Congress. It had already been decided that the President should have a veto power subject to being overruled by two thirds of the Congress. At this point in the discussion they upped this to three fourths, although it ultimately returned to the former figure. The Committee had proposed to grant Congress the power "to borrow money" and to "emit bills." This latter was frightening to delegates who had witnessed the debacle caused by unsupported paper money. Read of Delaware "thought the words, if not struck out, would be as alarming as the mark of the Beast in Revelations." They were struck out.

The important limitations of Congressional power had to do with commerce and, very incidentally, slavery. It should be pointed out that slavery was never a really important issue at the Constitutional Convention. It was the feeling of most of the delegates, North and South, that it would ultimately become extinct. Massachusetts had already forbidden it, and because Eli Whitney would not invent his gin until six years later, King Cotton did not yet rule. However, the three most southern states did not want to give the central government the right to control slavery, and three minor clauses in the Constitution protected their interests in this matter—although, in deference to those who objected to the institution on moral grounds, the words *slave* or *slavery* do not appear in the document. Abraham Lincoln would later theorize that "It was hoped that when it [the Constitution] should be read by intelligent and patriotic men, after the institution of slavery had passed from amongst us, there should be nothing on the face of the great charter of liberty suggesting that such a thing as Negro slavery had ever existed among us. They expected and intended that it should be put in the course of ultimate extinction."

When Georgia and North and South Carolina declared that they would never accept any plan "unless their right to import slaves be untouched," Ellsworth spoke for the majority when he said: "Let every state import what it pleases. The morality or wisdom of slavery are considerations belonging to the states themselves. What enriches a part enriches the whole, and the states are the best judges of their particular interest."

Another sectional difference had to do with export duties and navigation acts. The business of the South consisted entirely of exporting commodities. They were obviously opposed to export taxes and to any laws that would hinder them from sending their crops to any markets by the cheapest means. The North was concerned with ships and shipping. It wanted navigation laws that would favor American vessels. As Gouverneur Morris frankly expressed it, "These things may form a bargain among the northern and southern states."

The compromise was the acceptance of a proposition that Congress could not impose export taxes and would not prohibit, prior to 1808, "the migration or importation of such persons as the several states now existing shall think proper to admit." They did, however, impose a $10-a-head tax on newly imported slaves, which recognized their status as property. In return for this the South agreed to remove the provision that a two-thirds majority was required to pass navigation laws. This would make possible acts, favorable to the northern shipping interests, providing that American products be carried in American bottoms and that foreign shipping pay added fees.

To be absolutely accurate, the prohibition on export taxes was agreed to by the Convention before the slave-trade–navigation-act compromise was reached in committee, but they were really all based on the same principle; as was the clause that provided that a "person held to service in one state" who escaped into another "shall be delivered up on claim of the party to whom such service or labor is due." This would become the basis of the Fugitive Slave Law, on which was based the Dred Scott decision and other incidents leading to the Civil War.

Considering the extent to which the small states had fought for sovereignty, there was surprisingly little disagreement on the limitation of state authority specified by the Convention. They readily agreed that the states were to be prohibited from coining money, issuing bills of credit, making anything but specie legal tender, making treaties, laying duties, maintaining armies or navies, making agreements with other states, or engaging in war unless invaded. Most of these things had been provided for in the Articles of Confederation, except those having to do with money, which were new and based upon recent unhappy experiences with paper money.

If the extent of debate is any indication, the delegates seemed to have but little interest in the federal judiciary.

The provision that the legislature "might" establish inferior courts was reaffirmed on the basis, apparently, that most delegates believed that state courts should have primary jurisdiction in most cases, and the federal court should be purely appellate. For the time being the appointment of judges was left with the Senate. The extent of jurisdiction of the Supreme Court was further spelled out and extended to all cases involving ambassadors or public ministers; all cases involving maritime jurisdiction; and "controversies to which the United States shall be a party." It was also agreed that the writ of habeas corpus should not be suspended unless the public safety require such action.

In these days when the most publicized activities of the Supreme Court are its rulings on the constitutionality of new laws passed by Congress, it is interesting to note that nowhere in the Constitution is the court specifically granted this authority. There is no question that the framers of the Constitution assumed that the court should have this power. This is apparent from statements made by many of the delegates during the debate on the question of whether the court was to join with the President in the veto power. Perhaps Madison expressed it best when, after making the point that unless ratified by the people the Constitution would be merely a treaty, he continued: "A law violating a treaty ratified by a pre-existing law might be respected by the judges as a law, though an unwise or perfidious one. A law violating a Constitution established by the people themselves would be considered by the judges as null and void."

The Convention swept through the rest of the report of the Committee of Detail rather quickly, endorsing most of what had been recommended with little change, including interstate privileges such as the extradition of criminals and recognition of one state's laws and judicial proceedings by another and giving citizens of one state the privileges of citizens in the other states. The Convention accepted the committee's proposal that the Constitution could be amended if two thirds of the states voted for the amendment.

It had already been decided that the Constitution should be ratified by assemblies chosen by the people, but what constituted ratification had not been discussed. The first motion called for ratification by all thirteen states. This was quickly defeated—unanimous ratification of the Constitution was obviously impossible when one state would not even discuss the document. A motion that ten states be required for ratification was defeated by a small majority. Madison was in favor of putting the charter into effect if only seven states ratified. This was disapproved, and a proposal for nine states was finally accepted.

The point was raised that there was a Congress in existence that deserved some consideration. Approval by the dilatory Congress might take years, yet ignoring it entirely was too discourteous. It was decided to submit the document to the existing legislature with the recommendation that it be submitted to the conventions in the various states.

5

The Problem of a President

Perhaps the best way to explain how the Convention solved—or thought it solved—its most persistent problem is to start with the solution and work backward. Following is what the Constitution has to say about how the President shall be elected, before the system was modified by the twelfth amendment in 1804.

"Each State shall appoint, in such Manner as the Legislature thereof may direct, a Number of Electors, equal to the whole Number of Senators and Representatives to which the State may be entitled in the Congress: but no Senator or Representative, or Person holding an Office of Trust or Profit under the United States, shall be appointed an Elector.

"The Electors shall meet in their respective States, and vote by Ballot for two Persons, of whom one at least shall not be an inhabitant of the same State with themselves.

And they shall make a List of all the Persons voted for, and of the Number of Votes for each; which List they shall sign and certify, and transmit sealed to the Seat of Government of the United States, directed to the President of the Senate. The President of the Senate shall, in the Presence of the Senate and House of Representatives, open all the Certificates, and the Votes shall then be counted. The Person having the greatest Number of Votes shall be the President, if such Number be a Majority of the whole Number of Electors appointed; and if there be more than one who have such a Majority, and have an equal Number of Votes, then the House of Representatives shall immediately chuse by Ballot one of them for President; and if no Person have a Majority, then from the five highest on the List the said House shall in like Manner chuse the President. But in chusing the President, the Votes shall be taken by States, the Representation from each State having one Vote; A quorum for this Purpose shall consist of a Member or Members from two thirds of the States, and a Majority of all the States shall be necessary to a Choice. In every Case, after the Choice of the President, the Person having the greatest Number of Votes of the Electors shall be the Vice President. But if there should remain two or more who have equal Votes, the Senate shall chuse from them by Ballot the Vice President.

"The Congress may determine the Time of chusing the Electors, and the Day on which they shall give their Votes; which Day shall be the same throughout the United States."

The executive had been the subject of discussion, on and off, throughout the Convention. Each time the matter was discussed the functions of the executive became a little more definite. It had been decided that it would be one man who would have the power to execute the national laws, he would have limited veto power, he would be subject to impeachment, and he would have the right to make some appointments. The Committee of Detail had added that he should give information to Congress and could recommend legislation to that body; that he could convene Congress in the extraordinary session; that he was to be commander-in-chief of the army and navy; and that he should receive ambassadors and could grant pardons.

The powers of the executive were gradually getting more extensive. Obviously, he must not be merely a creature of the legislature. On the other hand, steps must be taken to assure that he would never become a monarch. The opinion of many delegates on the presidency was expressed a few weeks after the Convention by Baldwin of Georgia to President Ezra Stiles of Yale, who noted in his diary:

"As to a President, it appeared to be the Opinion of Convention, that he should be a Character respectable by the Nations as well as by the federal Empire. To this End that as much Power should be given him as could be consistent with guarding against all possibility of his ascending in a Tract of years or Ages to Despotism and absolute Monarchy;—of which all were cautious. Nor did it appear that any Members in Convention had the least Idea of insidiously laying the Foundation of a future Monarchy like the European or Asiatic Monarchies either antient or modern. But were unanimously guarded and firm against every Thing of this ultimate Tendency. Accordingly they meant to give considerable Weight as Supreme Executive, but fixt him dependent on the States at large, and at all times impeachable."

The subject of monarchy was one that lurked in all minds—a monarch was the only type of chief of state with which any of the delegates had had experience. There was a rumor outside the Convention during August that the delegates were considering a monarchy and that the second son of George III was to be invited to become King of the United States. There is no foundation for this, but evidence has been advanced that Gorham of Massachusetts had written to Prince Henry of Prussia in 1786, discussing the possibility of his becoming King of the United States. McHenry of Maryland claimed that his colleague Mercer had made a list of twenty delegates who favored some form of royal government, and John Jay wrote to Washington, "I am told that even respectable characters speak for a monarchial form of government." Even Franklin, in a codicil to his will written two years after the Convention, intimated that he would not be too opposed to a King George—if his last name was Washington. He wrote: "My fine crab-tree walking stick, with a gold head curiously wrought in the form of a cap of liberty, I give to my friend, and the friend of mankind, George Washington. If it were a scepter, he has merited it and would become it."

It seems that some delegates decided to take concerted action to stop the rumors, for there appears in several private letters written from Philadelphia a statement, on which the writers had obviously agreed, to the effect that, "Although we cannot, affirmatively, tell you what we are doing, we can, negatively, tell you what we are not doing —we never once thought of a king."

The manner of selecting the first President was complicated by the fact that all the delegates assumed that, regardless of the method of selection, Washington would be the man. What they had to do was create a system of selection that would apply at some distant date when there was no outstanding leader who rose above sectional and factional interests.

The proposal of the Committee of Detail—election by Congress—was entirely unsatisfactory. The Convention voted down a proposal for election by the people; voted down a proposal for election by electors selected by the people; and rejected by a tie vote the general proposition of election by electors. They then gave up, on the last day of August, and referred the matter to another committee. Wilson remarked: "This subject has greatly divided the house and will also divide people out of doors. It is in truth the most difficult of all on which we have had to decide."

On September 4, the committee came back with the proposal that was the basis for the system that was finally adopted. It suggested electors from each state equal in number to the total state representation in Congress, who could be selected in any manner the state saw fit but who would probably be appointed by the state legislatures. They would vote for two people, and unless one man had a majority of the total votes the Senate—not the House of Representatives—would select the President from the five leading candidates. The man who came in second would be Vice-President, and in case of a tie, the Senate would make the choice.

This was the first time that a Vice-President had been seriously proposed. He was very much of an afterthought and, said Williamson of North Carolina, who was a member of the Committee, "was not wanted. He was introduced only for the sake of a valuable mode of election which required two to be chosen at the same time." The committee proposed that the Vice-President be ex officio President of the Senate, and after some rather mild objections, this was approved—more or less on the grounds that if such an officer existed he should have something to do.

The committee also proposed the qualifications of the President; he should be at least thirty-five years of age, a resident of the country for fourteen years, and either native-born or a citizen of the United States at the time of the adoption of the Constitution. They also proposed added powers for the chief executive. With the "advice and consent" of the Senate he would make treaties and appoint ambassadors and judges of the Supreme Court. Treaties required approval by two thirds of the Senate.

After thinking it over a while, the Convention adopted the Committee recommendation with little change. In fact, the correspondence of some delegates gives the impression that they considered this complex method of selecting a chief executive as the Convention's greatest achievement, which would stand as a model for other countries.

There was some objection to the added power given the Senate to select a President in case no candidate had a majority. When it was proposed that the choice be shifted to the House of Representatives, with each state's contingent of congressmen having but one vote, this was immediately accepted. The original objection to electors—the expense of traveling to a meeting—was overcome by providing that they meet in their own states. It was remarked that by voting at the same time and at a great distance

from each other, "the great evil of cabal was avoided."
Nobody explained what the evils of "cabal" were. Perhaps
there was some thought of undercover deals or other forms
of corruption. Or there may have been an inkling, in the
minds of some delegates, that political parties might de-
velop. If so, this was never mentioned. Most of the delegates would have been aghast at the idea of the two-party
system, which, on the whole, has proved to be a most satisfactory means of operating a democratic government.

It was decided that the President should serve for four
years and be subject to re-election. Nothing was said about
a third term. The idea of providing for a President's council was turned down, but it was specified that the President
be empowered to require the written opinions of the head
of each executive department. This obviously contemplated
the existence of such departments with a single officer in charge of each who would form an advisory group to
the chief executive. Rather incidentally, the trial of cases
of impeachment was shifted from the Supreme Court to the
Senate.

Although it is not obvious on the face of it, the method
of selecting the President was another big-state–small-state
compromise. The electors would be more numerous from
the large states, and these states had an advantage in the
first step of selection. However, it was generally believed
that one man would seldom have a clear-cut majority of
the total electoral vote—always excepting Washington.
This would place the final choice in the hands of the
states: through the Senate in the Committee recommendation and in the lower house voting by states in the final
provision. Mason of Virginia said that he expected this to
happen "nineteen times in twenty." In short, it was ex-

pected that the large states would be dominant in the selection of five candidates from whom the final election
might be made by a group in which the small states had an
equal vote.

It was now the eighth of September. The Convention
was getting tired—it had been a long, hot summer. That
most of the delegates were finished with debate is evident
from these terse records from Madison's journal for that
day.

MR. WILSON and MR. DAYTON moved to strike out the clause
requiring two-thirds of the Senate for making treaties; on
which—[The journal then recorded the vote; nine states no,
one divided.]

MR. RUTLEDGE and MR. GERRY moved that "no treaty shall be
made without the consent of two-thirds of all the members
of the Senate," according to the example in the present
Congress.

MR. GORHAM. There is a difference in the case, as the President's consent will also be necessary in the new government.
On the question;—"[three states "aye," eight states "no"].

MR. SHERMAN moved that, "No treaty shall be made without
a majority of the whole number of the Senate."

MR. GERRY seconded him.

MR. WILLIAMSON. This will be less security than two-thirds,
as now required.

MR. SHERMAN. It will be less embarrassing.

On the question it was passed in the negative.

MR. MADISON moved that a quorum of the Senate consist of
two-thirds of all the members.

MR. GOUVERNEUR MORRIS. This will put it in the power of one
man to break up a quorum.

MR. MADISON. This may happen to any quorum.

On the question it passed in the negative.

And so it went, with motion after motion disposed of in
a matter of minutes, far different from the almost endless

wrangling of the past ten weeks. Everybody—or almost everybody—seemed to be in agreement, and a committee of five was appointed "to revise the style and arrange the articles which had been agreed to by the house." Johnson of Connecticut, Hamilton of New York, Gouverneur Morris of Pennsylvania, James Madison of Virginia, and Rufus King of Massachusetts were selected for this chore.

Gouverneur Morris apparently did the actual writing of the Constitution. At least he wrote Timothy Pickering, several years later, that the Constitution "was written by the fingers which write this letter." Madison confirmed this in a letter to Jared Sparks, President of Harvard, in which he said: "The finish . . . fairly belongs to the pen of Mr. Morris. . . . A better choice could not have been made, as the performance of the task proved. It is true that the state of the materials . . . was a good preparation . . . but there was a sufficient room for the talents and taste stamped by the author on the face of it."

Although the Committee on Style followed the resolutions of the Convention very closely in their draft, there is some evidence that Morris phrased the document, when he could, to favor his own ideas. He later admitted as much. In connection with the admission of new states, one of his pet projects, he wrote: "In wording the third section of the fourth article, I went as far as circumstances would permit to establish the exclusion [of new states on an equal basis]. Candor obliges me to add my belief that, had it been more pointedly expressed, a strong opposition would have been made."

A few delegates continued to argue to the bitter end. The percentages of votes needed to override a Presidential veto had been changed from two thirds to three quarters on a motion by Williamson. Now the gentleman from North Carolina wanted to reverse himself and change it back. Madison spoke against it, but the group no longer cared to listen to arguments belaboring minor points. They voted the change. Williamson also proposed that jury trials be specified in civil as well as criminal cases. He got few supporters. Mason, with his Virginia Bill of Rights in mind, proposed that there should be a similar section in the Constitution. Sherman spoke briefly against it, and it was voted down.

The Committee on Style presented their handiwork, in printed form, on September 13. It was well received, and the few hairsplitters who called for minute changes were generally indulged in the interests of completing the work, although some suggestions were turned down. Among these was a proposal that there should be a declaration for freedom of the press. It was decided that Congress had no power over the press and that such a declaration would be out of order. A proposal for a national university met a similar fate on the grounds that Congress would have jurisdiction over the seat of the government, where such a university would presumably be located, and could start one if they wanted to.

One matter that later assumed great importance was brought up at this time in a roundabout way. Benjamin Franklin proposed that Congress be given specific power to construct canals. Madison proposed to make this more general by authorizing Congress to make "internal improvements." There was considerable objection to this on the grounds that some might interpret it as authorizing Congress to start a bank; others might see in it a possibility of establishing commercial monopolies. The motion, put in terms of canals as being the most important internal improvements then visualized, was supported only by three states.

With its report the Committee on Style had submitted a letter of conveyal addressed to Congress. After pointing out the need for a stronger central government, and the difficulty of attaining this and at the same time protecting the independent sovereignty of each state, the letter continued:

"In all our deliberations on this subject, we kept steadily in our view that which appeared to us the greatest interest of every true American, the consolidation of our union, in which is involved our prosperity, felicity, safety, perhaps our national existence. This important consideration, seriously and deeply impressed on our minds, led each state in the Convention to be less rigid in points of inferior magnitude than might have been otherwise expected. And thus the Constitution which we now present is the result of a spirit of amity, and of that mutual deference and concession, which the peculiarity of our political situation rendered indispensable.

"That it will meet the full and entire approbation of every state is not, perhaps, to be expected. But each will doubtless consider, that, had her interest alone been consulted, the consequences might have been particularly disagreeable and injurious to others. That it is liable to as few exceptions as could reasonably have been expected, we hope and believe; that it may promote the lasting welfare of that country so dear to us all, and secure her freedom and happiness, is our most ardent wish."

After everything had been presumably agreed to, Virginia's Governor Edmund Randolph rose to speak "on the indefinite and dangerous power given by the Constitution to Congress, expressing the pain he felt at differing from the body of the Convention on the close of the great and awful subject of their labors, and anxiously wishing for some accommodating expedient which would relieve him from his embarrassments, made a motion importing, 'that amendments to the plan might be offered by the state conventions which should be submitted to, and finally decided on by another General Convention.' " Should this proposition be disregarded, it would, he said, be impossible for him to put his name to the instrument.

Fellow Virginian Mason supported Randolph and said that, unless a second Convention was provided for, he could neither give the Constitution his support nor vote for it in Virginia. All states voted no to Randolph's motion. Gerry of Massachusetts had already stated that he would not accept the document unless it provided for the assumption of state debts by the federal government.

On Saturday September 15, Madison noted tersely: "On the question to agree to the Constitution, as amended, all the states, aye. The Constitution was then ordered to be engrossed, and the house adjourned."

The refusal of three members to sign created a minor problem. In the interests of getting the document ratified it was highly desirable to present it as the unanimous recommendation of the Convention. Gouverneur Morris got around this slyly by writing a tailpiece, "Done in Convention, by the unanimous consent of *the States* present the 17th of September. . . . In Witness whereof we have hereunto subscribed our names." To assure the acceptance of this "weasel" he did not present it himself but handed it to Franklin, knowing that the respect of the delegates for the old sage would carry the proposition.

Franklin rose to the occasion, or rather, Wilson rose for him to read a speech that Franklin had prepared. He started by saying, "I confess that I do not entirely approve of this Constitution at present; but, sir, I am not sure I shall never approve it; for having lived long, I have experienced many instances of being obliged, by better information or fuller consideration, to change opinions even on important subjects, which I once thought right, but found to be other wise." He made the point that no man is infallible, which he illustrated with a story of an old lady who ended a dispute with her sister by saying, "But I meet with nobody but myself who is *always* in the right." He then continued:

"In these sentiments, sir, I agree to this Constitution, with all its faults—if they are such—because I think a general government necessary for us, and there is no form of government but what may be a blessing to the people, if well administered for a course of years, and can only end in despotism, as other forms have done before it, when the people shall become so corrupted as to need despotic government, being incapable of any other. . . . It therefore astonishes me, sir, to find this system approaching so near perfection as it does; and I think it will astonish our enemies, who are waiting with confidence to hear that our counsels are confounded like those of the builders of Babel, and that our States are on the point of separation, only to meet hereafter for the purpose of cutting one another's throats. Thus I consent, sir, to this Constitution, because I expect no better, and because I am not sure that it is not the best. The opinions I have had of its errors I sacrifice to the public good. . . . I hope, therefore, for our own sakes, as a part of the people, and for the sake of our posterity, that we shall act heartily and unanimously in recommending this Constitution, wherever our influence may extend, and turn our future thoughts and endeavors to the means of having it well administered.

"On the whole, sir, I cannot help expressing a wish that every member of the convention who may still have objections to it would with me on this occasion doubt a little of his own infallibility and, to make manifest our unanimity, put his name to this instrument."

Just as the question was to be put for the signing of the engrossed copy, Gorham of Massachusetts rose to propose that the number of inhabitants per representative in the lower house be decreased from 40,000 to 30,000. He surely would have been voted down unanimously except that, for some unaccountable reason, Washington spoke for the first and only time in the Convention. After remarking that his "situation had hitherto restrained him from offering his sentiments," he said, according to Madison, "he could not forbear expressing his wish that the alteration proposed might take place. . . . The smallness of the proportion of representatives had been considered, by many members of the Convention, an insufficient security for the rights and interests of the people. . . . and, late as the present moment was for admitting amendments, he thought this of so much consequence, that it would give him much satisfaction to see it adopted." Gorham's proposal was adopted unanimously.

Thirty-nine delegates then signed the new charter of American government. Madison's journal ends with this note:

"The Constitution being signed by all the members, except Mr. Randolph, Mr. Mason, and Mr. Gerry, who declined giving it the sanction of their names, the Convention dissolved itself by an adjournment *sine die*.

"Whilst the last members were signing, Dr. FRANKLIN, looking towards the president's chair, at the back of which a rising sun happened to be painted, observed to a few members near him, that the painters had found it difficult to distinguish, in their art, a rising from a setting sun. 'I have,' said he, 'often and often, in the course of the session, and the vicissitudes of my hopes and fears as to its issue, looked at that behind the president, without being able to tell whether it was rising or setting; but now, at length, I have the happiness to know that it is a rising, and not a setting sun.'"

The Final Compromise

When the Constitution of the United States issued from the State House in Philadelphia, it is not an exaggeration to say that it represented a bombshell. Although some delegates who left early may have intimated to close associates what was going on behind closed doors in the Quaker City, secrecy had, in the main, been well kept. It was generally believed that the Convention would recommend some amendments to the Articles of Confederation, that these would be acted on by the Congress and, if that body approved, would be submitted to the state legislatures for ratification.

Instead, the document that went to Congress with a polite letter from George Washington was an entirely new charter of government that superseded the old Articles and that, if ratified, would terminate the existence of the old Congress. Further, it specifically provided that neither the Congress nor the state legislatures were to have anything to say about its acceptance. Ratification was to be by conventions in each state whose members would be selected by the people in special elections.

Richard Henry Lee immediately rose to attack the document in Congress, calling for various changes before it was submitted for ratification. Congress refused to consider these proposals and sent the Constitution to the states without debate. This touched off a series of controversies in most of the states and the formation of Federalist and Antifederalist groups, which represented the embryos of the future two-party political system. The Nationalists of the Convention were now the Federalists.

Generally, the opposition to the Constitution was in terms of group interests rather than on sectional lines. Most debtors and small property owners were against this new system, which provided for sound money. This class had not been represented in the Convention, of which the members had been, almost exclusively, wealthy men. They were represented to a larger extent in the state legislatures, which were required to call the special conventions; and they would be well represented in these conventions. However, they were largely leaderless. Traditionally, leadership did not come from this group.

There was considerable opposition to the document on the part of the churches, particularly the Presbyterian and the Baptist. The Constitution said nothing about religion, and there was a fear that the lack of a provision against it might lead to some form of state religion.

Many state leaders were opposed to giving up any state power to the new government; some for selfish reasons having to do with their own positions, others because they sincerely thought that the strong central government would infringe on the rights of their individual states. Patrick Henry, for instance, wanted no government under which the great commonwealth of Virginia would lose any part of its political identity. As a case in point, he feared that the new federal government might make a treaty with Spain regarding the Mississippi, which would be injurious to the western part of his state.

There was a rather general fear that the central government would become an instrument of arbitrary power. This was heightened by the provision for Congressional control of the militia, which smacked of a standing army, widely feared as a potential arm of a despot. And where was the provision in the Constitution that would prevent the chief executive from using the Presidency as a stepping-stone to monarchy?

Principally, the demand was for a bill of rights, such as those that were embodied in most state constitutions, which specifically guaranteed the protection of certain freedoms and liberties for the individual.

This cry for a bill of rights came not only from the active Antifederalists. John Adams, who would become the first Federalist President, wrote from London to Thomas Jefferson in France: "What think you of a declaration of rights? Should not such a thing have preceded the model?" In his first expression of opinion on the Constitution to Adams, Jefferson said, "I confess there are things in it which stagger all my dispositions to subscribe to what such an assembly has proposed." Then he took quill in hand to tell James Madison what he liked and what he opposed in the document.

"I like much the general idea of framing a government

which should go on by itself peaceably, without needing continual recurrence to state legislatures. I like the organization of the government into legislative, judiciary, and executive. I like the power given the legislature to levy taxes, and for that reason solely approve of the greater house being chosen by the people directly. For though I think that a house chosen by them will be very illy qualified to legislate for the union, for foreign nations etc., yet this evil does not weigh against the good of preserving inviolate the fundamental principle that the people are not to be taxed but by representatives chosen immediately by themselves. I am captivated by the compromise of the opposite claims of the great and little states, of the latter to equal and the former a proportional influence. I am pleased too with the substitution of the method of voting by persons, instead of that of voting by states and I like the negative [veto power] given to the executive. . . . There are other good things of less moment.

"I will now add what I do not like. First the omission of a bill of rights providing clearly and without the aid of sophisms for freedom of religion, freedom of the press, protection against standing armies, restriction against monopolies, the eternal and unremitting force of the habeas corpus, and trials by jury. . . . The second feature I dislike, and greatly dislike, is the abandonment in every instance of the necessity of rotation in office, and most particularly in the case of the President. Experience concurs with reason in concluding that the first magistrate will always be re-elected if the Constitution permits it. He is then an officer for life."

Jefferson reiterated his desire for a bill of rights, saying, "A bill of rights is what the people are entitled to against every government on earth, general or particular [that is, federal or state] and what no government should refuse or rest on inferences." He advanced a rather wily plan for accomplishing his purpose. "I would advocate it [the Constitution] warmly," he wrote, "till nine [states] should have adopted, and then as warmly take the other side to convince the remaining four that they ought not to come into it till the declaration of rights is annexed to it. By these means we should secure all the good of it and procure so respectable an opposition as would induce the accepting states to offer a bill of rights. This would be the happiest turn the thing could take."

The Antifederalists had another plan: to submit the Constitution for discussion and then call for another national convention to revise it in accordance with proposals developed during discussion in the states. Mason and Randolph of Virginia had proposed this in the Convention, and Mason, together with Richard Henry Lee, became the most active pamphleteers for the Antifederalist point of view. Lee suggested that "the plan for us to pursue will be to propose the necessary amendments and express our willingness to adopt it with the amendments; and to suggest the calling of a new convention for the purpose of considering them." Patrick Henry took this proposal before the Virginia House of Delegates and had it embodied in the act that authorized the calling of that state's ratification convention.

As with the question of state's rights, some of those who advocated a second convention before ratification were undoubtedly sincere. On the other hand, many who proposed this were certainly hoping that a second convention, with delegates burdened down with specific instructions from state bodies, would be able to agree on nothing.

Washington, watching from Mount Vernon, was convinced that most of the Antifederalist literature was merely designed to frighten people. "Every attempt to amend the Constitution at this time is, in my opinion, idly vain," he wrote. Alexander Hamilton insisted that the Antifederalists were simply demagogues whose arguments scarcely deserved rebuttal. "It is the plan of men of this stamp to frighten the people with idle bugbears in order to mould them to their own purposes," he charged. "The unceasing cry of these designing croakers is, 'My friends, your liberty is invaded.' "

A bill of rights became the cause celebre of the controversy. In Pennsylvania James Wilson, although a long-time champion of the rights of the people, insisted that it was not necessary and did not belong in the Constitution. He pointed out that the powers of the government came from positive grants that were specifically stated in the Constitution, and that every power not granted to Congress was reserved by the people. "This distinction being recognized," he continued, "will furnish an answer to those who think the omission of a bill of rights a defect in the proposed Constitution; for it would be superfluous and absurd to have stipulated with a federal body of our own creation that we should enjoy those privileges of which we are not divested either by the intention or the act that has brought that body into existence."

Hamilton devoted the next to the last of the eighty-five essays that comprise *The Federalist* to a dissertation on why a bill of rights was not only unnecessary in the Constitution but would be, in fact, undesirable and injurious to the liberties of the people. Some of his rather specious reasoning in this area is indicated by his argument dealing with freedom of the press:

"I . . . affirm that bills of rights, in the sense and to the extent in which they are contended for, are not only unnecessary in the proposed Constitution but would even be dangerous. They would contain various exceptions to powers not granted; and, on this very account, would afford a colorable pretext to claim more than were granted. For why declare that things shall not be done which there is no power to do? Why, for instance, should it be said that the liberty of the press shall not be restrained, when no power is given by which restrictions may be imposed? I will not contend that such provision would confer a regulating power; but it is evident that it would furnish, to men disposed to usurp, a plausible pretense for claiming that power. They might urge, with a semblance of reason, that the Constitution ought not to be charged with the absurdity of providing against the abuse of an authority which was not given, and that the provision against restraining the liberty of the press afforded a clear implication that a power to prescribe proper regulations concerning it was intended to be vested in the national government. This may serve as a specimen of the numerous handles which would be given to the doctrine of constructive powers by the indulgence of an unjudicious zeal for bills of rights."

The extent of the discussion on ratification might give the impression that it was a subject for every tongue in the thirteen states. Actually, the situation was quite different. It is safe to say that a goodly number of Americans, at that time, heard little of the Constitution and that most did not read it. The document was discussed extensively in the country's ninety-three newspapers, but these circulated largely in the cities. In New Hampshire only 400 copies of the Constitution were printed; in Maryland, with 25,000 voters, only 2,000 copies were printed. As a result only 6,000 voted in that state, and of these about 4,000 were from the more populous sections.

Generally speaking, the ratifying conventions did not represent all of the people equally; city folk had more representation than rural areas. In New York, for instance, twenty-three of the sixty-three delegates were from New York City and Westchester County, although these areas had little more than one quarter of the state's population. To a lesser extent this was true in connection with the western areas of Massachusetts, Pennsylvania, and Virginia. Since the vote was very close in three of these states, and Antifederalist sentiment was stronger in rural areas, the decision might have been different had the population been represented on a proportional basis.

The three states in which the situation was most critical were Virginia, Massachusetts, and New York; the first because they were two of the three biggest and New York because of its location. Despite the fact that the union would become established with only nine states ratifying, a solid union would be inconceivable without New York and with the four states north of her being isolated by their recalcitrant neighbor.

Delaware was the first state to ratify, unanimously, on December 7, 1787, less than three months after the Philadelphia Convention. Meanwhile, a brisk fight was shaping in Pennsylvania. Here the ratifying convention had been called for November 20, and the Antifederalists maintained that this early date was the result of a nefarious plot by the Federalists to stifle full discussion. Both sides waged war through the press. Was the document "to be so hastily adopted or rejected that it cannot admit of revision?" cried a writer who signed himself "Old Whig." And, he added, "It will not be done without a careful attention to the framing of a bill of rights." This rabid Antifederalist abolished the Federalist argument that the new government would not challenge freedom of religion by thundering, "They are idiots who trust their future security to the whim of the present hour. . . . What is there in the new proposed Constitution to prevent his [a conscientious objector's] being dragged like a Prussian soldier to the camp and there compelled to bear arms?" This, of course, was aimed at the pacifistic Quakers. Without a bill of rights, said the Old Whig, all personal rights would depend "on the will and the pleasure" of their rulers.

Federalist writers replied with logic, sarcasm and some venom. "An American Citizen" pointed out that there was no bill of rights in the Articles of Confederation, and personal rights had never been usurped under the old government. He noted that nothing was said in the Constitution about the privilege of eating and drinking, but doubted that any man was seriously afraid that his right to dine was endangered by the document's silence on these points. No mention of personal rights was necessary in the federal charter, he said, "because they are already provided for by the state constitutions."

Most of the writing was in a more serious vein, as pamphlets and articles for both sides arrived from other states and were reproduced in the local press. The Federal press quoted "Landholder" and "Publius"; the Antifederalist papers reprinted George Clinton's "Cato," Richard

Henry Lee's "Federal Farmer," and Mason's "Objections."

Lee's "Federal Farmer" seemed to have most influence in the rural areas of western Pennsylvania, where the strong Antifederalist sentiment that would one day produce the Whisky Rebellion already existed. He concentrated on the danger of a standing army and the limitation of jury trials and made the point that the few allusions to personal rights in the Constitution were a half-hearted admission that a full bill of rights should be included that spelled out the whole catalog of personal liberties; freedom of religion, jury trials, a prohibition on unreasonable warrants of search and seizure, freedom of the press—all these were essential in a national charter that would serve "for ages and millions yet unborn."

James Wilson answered these arguments in a speech to the newly organized Pennsylvania convention by pointing out that five states had no bills of rights in their constitutions: South Carolina, New Jersey, New York, Connecticut, and Rhode Island. (He could have added Georgia.) Citizens of these states had never felt this lack. This was rather contradictory reasoning, because the Federalists were making their main defense against the claim for a bill of rights on the grounds that these rights *were* guaranteed by state constitutions.

The western Antifederalists then offered the convention fifteen proposed amendments, representing a bill of rights, which were voted down, forty-six to twenty-three. The Constitution as it stood was then ratified by the Pennsylvania convention by an identical vote. The Antifederalists seceded and called a rump convention of their own to issue a minority report. News of ratification was greeted at Carlisle, Pennsylvania, with a riot and a pamphlet that raised the question of whether Pennsylvania ought not to reward the Federalists "with a suit of tar and feathers or a hempen necklace."

New Jersey and Georgia quickly followed Pennsylvania in ratifying with little discussion, and both unanimously. Federalist leaders in Connecticut had called an early convention, before opposition could fully organize. They were fortunate that Oliver Ellsworth and Roger Sherman were among them, two of the staunchest delegates from the Philadelphia Convention. Writing as "The Landholder," Ellsworth sought to demolish James Mason's "Objections," claiming that Mason had refused to sign the Constitution only because his motion for a two-thirds majority on navigation acts had failed to pass and that the rest of his objections were window dressing. He admitted that freedom of the press was not mentioned in the Constitution, but added, "Nor is liberty of conscience, or of matrimony, or of burial of the dead, but it is enough that Congress have no power to prohibit either, and can have no temptation."

Writing as "A Countryman," Roger Sherman also denounced the demand for a bill of rights, saying that those who were urging it had reached "the sublimity of *nonsense* and *alarm*." He added, "The only real security you can have for all your important rights must be in the nature of your government." The records of the Connecticut convention are meager, but there was apparently no formal demand for a bill of rights before it ratified, on January 9, 1788, by a vote of 128 to 40.

Meanwhile, the first really close fight was shaping in Massachusetts. During the first month of debate in its convention it seemed very likely that this key state would reject the Constitution. The Federalist leaders numbered Rufus King and Nathaniel Gorham, from the Philadelphia Convention, and Theophilus Parsons.

The most active leaders among the Antifederalists were not so prominent nor, at first, so vocal. They believed that they had a majority and let the Federalists carry the fight. And they had two big pluses on their side. John Hancock, president of the convention, was the richest man in New England; but even before the Revolution he had been something of a maverick. Now he was known to have distinct Antifederalist leanings; as was old Samuel Adams, another of the delegates whose prewar contributions to the fight for independence made his name still a power in Massachusetts. Of a strong central government, Samuel Adams had written, "The seeds of aristocracy began to spring even before the conclusion of our struggle for the natural rights of man, seeds which, like a canker worm, lie at the root of free governments."

Realizing their weakness, the Federalists offered a compromise. Theophilus Parsons drafted a set of recommended amendments, and the Federalists gave them to Hancock to propose as his own handiwork, to be forwarded with the ratified Constitution. The claim has been made that Hancock was offered a "deal" to support the Federalists. If Virginia did not ratify he would be nominated as President of the United States, and if the southern state did come in, he would be nominated as Vice-President. There is no valid evidence to confirm that his support of the proposed Federalist amendments was based upon this.

Adams rose to support the amendments offered by Hancock. When some of the Antifederalists continued to call for a bill of rights, Adams made a proposal that virtually represented such a bill, then, according to one delegate, endeavored to withdraw it, and finally voted against it. Amidst this confusion, Massachusetts ratified the Constitution on February 6, 1788 by a vote of 187 to 186—a switch of ten votes would have killed it.

With the ratification went recommended amendments dealing with reservation to the states of powers not delegated to Congress; restrictions on Congress in regulating elections; a requested prohibition from levying direct taxes and creating monopolies; and reference to grand jury indictments and jury trials in certain civil cases. There was no mention of freedom of conscience, freedom of the press, and freedom of speech. This was not a bill of rights; but it set a precedent for other states to ratify with proposed amendments.

New Hampshire had convened on the heels of Massachusetts, and the Federalists were confident of victory until it became evident that many delegates from rural areas had been pledged by their constituents to vote against the Constitution. This, plus express riders carrying the news of the close vote in Massachusetts, decided the Federalist leaders to push through a vote for adjournment in the hope that time and events would make the people more amenable.

The scene shifted to Maryland. Here Luther Martin, who had been the most vociferous, if not the most able, of the opponents of a strong central government at Philadelphia, was still crusading against the Constitution, supported by Samuel and Jeremiah Chase and William Paca. But there was a strange apathy in Maryland, as evidenced by the fact that only one quarter of those franchised bothered to vote for delegates. Despite Antifederalist thunder the Maryland convention ratified by a vote of sixty-three to eleven. The defeated minority issued a report demanding amendments.

South Carolina was next to convene. Rumors from the north were rife in the southern press, including one that Rhode Island had called a convention that would almost certainly ratify. Actually, the Rhode Island legislature, instead of authorizing a convention, had submitted the Constitution to town meetings, which had repudiated the document by a decisive vote of 2,708 to 237.

In the discussion on a bill of rights in South Carolina, young Charles Pinckney added a new comment. He noted that bills of rights usually started with some such statement as "all men are created equal." South Carolina, he said, would "make that declaration with very bad grace when a large part of our property consists of men who were actually born slaves." It was thought that the decision would be close here; the motion in the legislature to call a ratification convention had been passed by only one vote—76 to 75. However, the convention ratified by a vote of 149 to 73, although one delegate, Patrick Dollard, warned that his constituents would resist the Constitution until "your standing army, like Turkish janizaries enforcing despotic laws, must ram it down their throats with the points of bayonets." Here, as in Massachusetts and Maryland, ratification was accompanied by recommended amendments.

During the eight months since the Constitutional Convention had presented its handiwork, eight states had ratified. Only one more was needed to put the charter of government into effect. But the situation was not quite so simple as this would make it appear. Neither New York nor Virginia had ratified, and regardless of what the Constitution said, union would not be a reality without both of these states. By this time Antifederalists in New York and Virginia had organized the "Federal Republican Committee" and were sparing neither effort nor money to promote opposition to a strong central government. Also, in those states that had ratified, there was still an active resistance movement. Rioting continued in western Pennsylvania. Strong, and in some cases venomous, pamphlets poured from the Antifederalist press. The General Baptist Committee met in Virginia and discussed whether the new Constitution "made sufficient provision for the secure enjoyment of religious liberty; on which, it was agreed unanimously, that, in the opinion of the general committee, it did not." Franklin, as always the pourer of oil, wrote from what would be his deathbed, "Popular opposition to a public measure is no proof of its impropriety, even tho' the opposition be excited and headed by men of distinction."

The flood of amendments that had started in Massachusetts had given pause to some Federalist leaders. James Madison felt that they were a blemish on the ratification but that those of Massachusetts were "in the least offensive form." When news of Massachusetts' action reached France, Jefferson's busy quill penned a revision of his previous strategy. Still adamant for a bill of rights, he now declared: "If the states which were to decide after her [Massachusetts] should all do the same, it is impossible but that they must obtain the essential amendments. It will be more difficult, if we lose this instrument, to recover what is good in it than to correct what is bad after we adopt it."

In this atmosphere, New Hampshire reconvened. Here,

as in South Carolina, the slavery issue was raised, this time by an Antifederalist, Joshua Atherton, who claimed that by voting for the Constitution "we become consenters to, and partakers in, the sin and guilt of this abominable traffic, at least for a certain period, without any positive stipulation that it should even then be brought to an end." The extent of the emotion that had been aroused by the Constitution is evident from a letter penned in New Hampshire by Nicholas Gilman, Federalist delegate to the Philadelphia Convention. James Mason and Patrick Henry were among the most vocal Antifederalists. Of them Gilman wrote, "Had it been pleasing to the Preserver of Man, in the superabundance of his tender mercies, to have removed P——y with M——n to the regions of darkness, I am induced to think that the new system of government would have been adopted—but the delay in our back-sliding state has rendered it more doubtful in my mind than it has been at any period since the conception of the plan."

Despite Gilman's pessimism, New Hampshire became the ninth state to ratify, on June 21, 1788, by a vote of 57 to 46. There were recommended amendments having to do with a standing army, the public quartering of troops, and an assurance that Congress would make "no laws touching on religion, or to infringe the rights of conscience."

In Virginia, three titans led the opposition to the Constitution: Patrick Henry, James Mason, and Richard Henry Lee. Governor Edmund Randolph had refused to sign the document in Philadelphia, but had since talked like a Federalist; he could not be counted in either camp. Washington remained aloof at Mount Vernon. When he sent a copy of the document to Lafayette, he had written:

"It is now a child of Fortune, to be fostered by some and buffeted by others. What will be the general opinion on, or reception of, is not for me to decide, nor shall I say anything for or against it." However, Washington was believed to favor amendments. When urged to affirm or deny this he refused; but he did write to Lafayette that "there was not a member of the Convention, I believe, who had the least objection to what is contended for by the advocates of a *Bill of Rights and Tryal by Jury.*"

From France Jefferson continued to send advice to his disciple Madison; none of it was very helpful but all of it recommended a bill of rights. In fighting for the adoption of the Constitution as written, slim, young James Madison was facing gigantic competition, and even he was beginning to waver. Before the Virginia convention opened he conceded, "Recommended alterations are the only ground that occurs to me."

Among the Antifederalist leadership Lee was willing to be somewhat conciliatory. He proposed a plan to Mason under which the convention would recommend amendments and allow the new Congress two years to bring them into being. He insisted that there must be "a just security given to civil liberty," but felt that his plan would restore harmony, quiet the opposition, and avoid "risking the convulsion of conventions."

But Patrick Henry was in no mood for conciliation or compromise; and, next to Washington, Henry was the most respected Virginian. The lazy lawyer and fiery orator who had thrilled prewar patriots with "Give me liberty or give me death" and "If *this* be treason make the most of it" was still in his old form when he rose on the floor of the convention to denounce every aspect of the new charter of government, of which he said:

"Here is a resolution as radical as that which separated us from Great Britain. It is radical in this transition; our rights and privileges are endangered, and the sovereignty of the states will be relinquished; and cannot we plainly see that this is actually the case? The rights of conscience, trial by jury, liberty of the press, all your immunities and franchises, all pretensions to human rights and privileges, are rendered insecure, if not lost, by this change, so loudly talked of by some, and inconsiderately by others. Is this tame relinquishment of rights worthy of freemen? Is it worthy of that manly fortitude that ought to characterize republicans? It is said eight states have adopted this plan. I declare that if twelve states and a half had adopted it, I would, with manly firmness, and in spite of an erring world, reject it. You are not to inquire how your trade may be increased, nor how you are to become a great and powerful people, but how your liberties can be secured; for liberty ought to be the direct end of your government. . . .

"Will the abandonment of your most sacred rights tend to the security of your liberty? Liberty. The greatest of all earthly blessings—give us that precious jewel, and you may take every thing else. . . . Perhaps an invincible attachment to the dearest rights of man may, in these refined, enlightened days, be deemed old-fashioned; if so, I am contented to be so. I say, the time has been when every pulse of my heart beat for American liberty, and which, I believe, had a counterpart in the breast of every true American."

Henry hammered on the need for a bill of rights throughout the entire convention, speaking early and often; one of his speeches lasted seven hours. Madison accused him of attempting "to spin out the session" in order to tire the delegates into adjournment. It was obvious that the Federalists were willing to concede to ratification with recommended subsequent amendments, but this did not please Henry. He did not trust Federalist promises, and he was convinced that, regardless of the votes of conventions, the people as a whole had no more faith in the proposed new government than he had. "I believe that the great body of yeomanry are in decided opposition to it," he declaimed. "These men never will part with their political opinions. . . . Subsequent amendments will not do for men of this cast. . . .

"Have gentlemen no respect to the actual disposition of the people in the adopting states? Look at Pennsylvania and Massachusetts. These two great states have raised as great objections to that government as we do. There was a majority of only nineteen in Massachusetts. We are told that only ten thousand were represented in Pennsylvania, although seventy thousand had a right to be represented. Is not this a serious thing? Is it not worth while to turn your eyes, for a moment, from subsequent amendments to the situation of your country? Can you have a lasting union in these circumstances? It will be in vain to expect it. But if you agree to previous amendments, you shall have union, firm and solid."

To this Madison replied: "I am persuaded that the gentlemen who contend for previous amendments are not aware of the dangers which must result. Virginia, after having made opposition, will be obliged to recede from it. Might not the nine states say, with a great deal of propriety, 'It is not proper, decent, or right, in you, to demand that we should reverse what we have done. Do as we have done; place confidence in us, as we have done in one another; and then we shall freely, fairly, and dispassionately consider and investigate your propositions, and endeavor to gratify your wishes. But if you do not do this, it is more reasonable that you should yield to us than we to you. You cannot exist without us; you must be a member of the Union. . . .'

"As far as his amendments are not objectionable, or unsafe, so far they may be subsequently recommended—not because they are necessary, but because they can produce no possible danger, and may gratify some gentlemen's wishes. But I never can consent to his previous amendments, because they are pregnant with dreadful dangers."

This interchange between Henry and Madison was followed by a vote on the question of previous amendments, including a bill of rights. It was lost, 88 to 80. Then, on June 26, 1788, the Virginia convention ratified the Constitution and appointed a committee to draft proposed amendments. They prepared a list of forty, including a bill of rights copied from the Virginia constitution, and a statement enjoining Virginia's delegation to the new Congress to work for their adoption.

News of the Virginia ratification was a blow to the Antifederalists in New York, who were led by the state's governor, George Clinton. The Clinton forces were more interested in maintaining the status quo in government than in a bill of rights; under the Confederation New York collected very lucrative impost duties, which went directly into the state treasury. The New York Antifederalists had hoped that a demand from Virginia for a second convention or previous amendments would permit them to suspend all action on ratification.

The New York Federalists had the strongest leadership of any state; Alexander Hamilton, John Jay, and Robert Livingston, all from New York City. Upstate New York was strongly Antifederalist, and it believed that at least two thirds of the delegates to the convention were Antifederalist in sentiment. New York's final ratification by a three-vote majority is generally attributed to the political skill of Alexander Hamilton.

Hamilton surely deserves the major credit for the series of essays on the Constitution that are known collectively as *The Federalist*. These pieces, of which there were eighty-five in all, started to appear in the New York *Independent Gazette,* over the signature "Publius," in October, 1787, about a month after the adjournment of the Constitutional Convention. They were published at the rate of three or four a week, were widely reprinted, and appeared first in book form in March, 1788, after six states had ratified.

James Madison and John Jay wrote some numbers of *The Federalist,* and there has been, since the dawn of the nineteenth century, a controversy as to who wrote what—a dispute that surely will never be settled. There is no doubt that Jay wrote five, Madison fourteen, Hamilton fifty-one, and three were by Madison and Hamilton jointly. The authorship of twelve is in doubt; they were claimed by both Hamilton and Madison in various lists that each prepared, or gave verbally to friends, some time after the event. Although it is dangerous to make even a conditional statement, most authorities seem to be willing to credit the twelve disputed numbers to Hamilton.

The first of *The Federalist* essays, addressed to "The

People of the State of New York," said:

"After an unequivocal experience of the inefficiency of the subsisting federal government, you are called upon to deliberate on a new Constitution for the United States of America. The subject speaks its own importance; comprehending in its consequences nothing less than the existence of the UNION, the safety and welfare of the parts of which it is composed, the fate of an empire in many respects the most interesting in the world. It has been frequently remarked that it seems to have been reserved to the people of this country, by their conduct and example, to decide the important question, whether societies of men are really capable or not of establishing good government from reflection and choice, or whether they are forever destined to depend for their political constitutions on accident and force. If there be any truth in the remark, the crisis at which we are arrived may with propriety be regarded as the era in which that decision is to be made; and a wrong election of the part we shall act may, in this view, deserve to be considered as the general misfortune of mankind."

Subsequent papers analyzed, in great detail, the dangers of the lack of union; the advantages of a strong central government; the weaknesses of the Confederation; the manner in which the proposed Constitution met the present need; and a detailed review of every aspect of the new charter and the government proposed by it.

It is probably safe to say that *The Federalist* had little to do with securing the ratification of the Constitution. It is equally safe to say that it is one of the most important works on political science ever produced in the United States. Max Farrand says that the essays in *The Federalist* form "the most important commentary on the Constitution, making what is regarded as one of America's greatest books." Certainly *The Federalist* has been used more widely than any other source, by jurists, lawyers, historians, and scholars to interpret what the Constitution meant to the men who framed it.

But the New York delegates who met at Poughkeepsie on June 17, 1788, were not interested in political science. They were concerned with taxation, and talked for two weeks about the loss to their state under the new system. True, one delegate, Thomas Tredwell, spoke for a bill of rights, saying that "a government is like a mad horse which, notwithstanding all the curb you can put upon him, will sometimes run away with his rider." Just as a man would deserve a broken neck who rode such a horse, so should the people deserve oppression if they did not insist on limitations upon this proposed government.

Word from Virginia shifted the pattern of debate. Clinton called for conditional amendments on a large scale. Melancton Smith called for ratification "on condition," which would permit the state to withdraw from the compact if amendments were not added within a certain time. John Jay felt that the Antifederalists were running for cover and wrote Washington that they would settle for recommended amendments, adding, "The ground for *rejection* therefore seems to be entirely deserted." Hamilton was not so sure that the Federalists could carry anything better than a conditional ratification and was willing to "concur in rational recommendations."

The final result, after the Federalists had lost a motion to adjourn to gain time, was a rather strange compromise. The Antifederalist ranks split when Samuel Jones proposed that the idea of conditional amendments be dropped and that New York should ratify "in full confidence" that other states would accept the New York amendments—without saying what the state should do if they did not. The Federalists then offered a concession; they would agree to a circular letter that would be sent out to the states, suggesting another federal convention. Next day the Constitution, with a recommended bill of rights, was ratified by a vote of 30 to 27.

Nothing much came of the circular letter—only Virginia, North Carolina, and Rhode Island answered it. Washington felt that it was designed to "set everything afloat again." Madison saw it "as the signal for united exertions in pursuit of early amendments." James Mason saw in it the last hope of the Antifederalists and believed that if another convention was held the following spring there was still hope for "proper and safe amendments."

North Carolina called its convention in July, 1788. Here the principal issue was "cheap money versus sound money," plus demands by Baptists and Presbyterians for religious guarantees and a demand for a second federal convention. A vote on a Federalist proposal for ratification with recommended amendments was defeated, 184 to 84. The convention then adjourned after adopting a resolution to the effect that North Carolina was in a state of friendly suspension from the union, and it was therefore improper to either ratify or reject the Constitution.

The Union could function without North Carolina and Rhode Island, at least for a while. These states did finally ratify in November, 1789, and May, 1790, respectively. But, in the meantime, the Constitution had gone into effect on March 4, 1789, the new, two-house legislature had been created, and George Washington had made his long, slow ride to New York to become the first President.

The point has been made that the Constitution was ratified by representatives of a minority of the American people. This is undoubtedly true; the rural areas and particularly the western areas of some states were not proportionately represented. The framers of the document were seeking to establish a better system of government for their fellow men; but there is reason to doubt that the majority of their fellow men, at the time, agreed that this was a better system of government. In the graphic words of John Adams, the Constitution "was extorted from the grinding necessities of a reluctant people."

The point is also made that the Constitution might not have been ratified except for Washington and Franklin. They did nothing to secure its ratification; they were merely present at the Convention that drafted it. The *Pennsylvania Packet* indicated a widespread attitude when it editorialized, "The arguments . . . most insisted upon in favor of the proposed Constitution are that if the plan is not a good one it is impossible that either General Washington or Doctor Franklin would have recommended it." James Monroe summarized this more tersely to Jefferson when he wrote, "Be assured General Washington's influence carried the government."

7

The Finished Fabric

As a young man, John Marshall was a rather silent member of the Virginia convention that ratified the Constitution. Forty-five years later he was a great Chief Justice of the Supreme Court, who had done more than any one man to interpret it to sustain the theory of a strong central government. It was then that he wrote, in an opinion from the bench, his recollection of how the bill of rights in the Constitution had come into being. The Chief Justice recalled:

"Serious fears were extensively entertained that those powers which the patriot statesmen . . . deemed essential to union, and to the attainment of those invaluable objects for which union was sought, might be exercised in a manner dangerous to liberty. . . . In almost every convention by which the constitution was adopted, amendments to guard the abuse of power were recommended. . . . In compliance with a sentiment thus generally expressed, to quiet fears thus extensively entertained, amendments were proposed by the required majority in congress, and adopted by the states."

In view of the bitterness and furor of debate at the time this seems rather an uninspired description of the birth of the bill of rights; but it does cover the salient points—a concession by the proponents of a strong central government to what seemed to be the will of the people. However, when the heavily Federalist first Congress met in April, 1789—a quorum was not present in March—it was not at all certain that they would honor the implied promises of the conventions.

The Senate immediately busied itself with a proper title for the President. Its speaker, John Adams, had proposed to designate the chief executive "His Highness the President of the United States and Protector of Their Liberties," which caused Franklin to comment that the Vice-President was "always an honest man, often a wise one, but sometimes, and in some things, absolutely out of his senses."

The lower house promptly concerned itself with the fascinating subject of how to raise money by levying import duties. Nobody seemed very anxious to take up this subject of amendments to the new Constitution—nobody, that is, but James Madison.

While the government was being organized, Madison had a lengthy correspondence with Jefferson on the subject. He wrote: "My own opinion has always been in favor of a bill of rights. . . . At the same time I have never thought the omission a material defect, nor been anxious to supply it even by subsequent amendments for any other reason than that it is desired by others. I have not viewed it in an important light—." He then proceeded to give Jefferson four reasons why a bill of rights was not important, and followed this with three reasons why a bill of rights *was* important, principally that "Political truths declared in that solemn manner acquire by degrees the character of fundamental maxims of free government, and as they become incorporated with the national sentiment, counteract the impulses of interest and passion."

For a time it seemed that Madison's opinion would be of little consequence, because he would have no part in the new government. He was defeated for the Senate by Richard Henry Lee, backed by Patrick Henry. In a move to keep him out of the lower house James Monroe, who already had a popular following, had been advanced to oppose him on an Antifederalist ticket, and a whispering campaign was started that Madison did not see any need for a single amendment to the Constitution. Madison made a hurried trip back to his district and issued a statement that "It is my sincere opinion that the Constitution ought to be revised, and that the first Congress meeting under it ought to prepare and recommend to the states for ratification the most satisfactory provisions for all essential rights, particularly the rights of the conscience in the fullest latitude, the freedom of the press, trials by jury, security against warrants, etc." Madison won his seat, and now he felt that his personal pledge and the compromises promised by other Federalists should be honored.

Virginia and New York were still calling for another convention to consider extensive changes in the Constitution when Madison announced that he would introduce the subject of amendments on May 25. At that time the House was still wrangling over money, and it was two weeks

later before Madison could get a hearing for his proposed
amendments. These were nine in number, based largely
on the Declaration of Rights in the Virginia constitution,
and it was Madison's proposal that they be incorporated
into the body of the Constitution at appropriate places.

The Congress was still in no hurry to consider amendments. Madison was one of a few who was adamant that
the legislature be committed to this course, and his proposal, together with the scores of amendments that had
been recommended by the various states, was submitted to
a special committee, strongly Federalist in its make-up.
The committee virtually ignored all other suggested
amendments and recommended Madison's proposal, with
little change, to the House. Here his nine points were
amplified into seventeen, and his suggestion for incorporating the amendments into the body of the Constitution was dropped in favor of a proposal for tacking them
on to the end.

Madison did some capable political tight-rope walking
in shepherding through the House what would become the
Bill of Rights. In the public mind the Bill of Rights is
more often associated with Thomas Jefferson than with
any other Founding Father. Orators at Jefferson Day din-
ners have long discoursed on "Thomas Jefferson's Bill of
Rights." Actually, Jefferson had little to do with the
famous charter of personal liberty except to write letters
from France saying that he favored it. Although it may be
an exaggeration to talk of "Mr. Madison's Constitution," it
would not be inappropriate to style the first amendments
"Mr. Madison's Bill of Rights."

What Madison proposed would satisfy public opinion,
yet be acceptable to all but the extremists on either side.

He pointed out that his changes would not "endanger the beauty of the government in any one important feature, even in the eyes of its most sanguine admirers," but that they would go far toward making "the Constitution better in the opinion of those who opposed it, without weakening its frame or abridging its usefulness. . . . We act the part of wise and liberal men who make such alterations as shall produce that effect."

Debate in the House droned on, with the same arguments against a bill of rights that had been repeated since 1787—and some silly new ones. Samuel Livermore, for instance, objected to the "cruel and unusual punishments" clause, because, he pointed out, it was sometimes necessary to cut off the ears of criminals, and some people might think that this was cruel.

Finally, the seventeen points adopted by the House were referred to the Senate, where it was promptly proposed that the whole matter be postponed until the next session of Congress. Those who argued for this maintained that a little experience was needed to indicate that amendments were necessary; to which Richard Henry Lee snorted, "As if experience were necessary to prove the propriety of those great principles of civil liberty which the wisdom of the ages has found to be necessary barriers against the encroachments of power in the hand of frail man."

When the Senate did get around to debating the House bill, in September, 1789, they reduced the seventeen proposed amendments to twelve, mainly by cutting verbiage and combining several points. For instance, Madison's suggested third and fourth articles were merged into a form very close to the final version of the all-important first amendment: "Congress shall make no law establishing articles of faith, or a mode of worship, or prohibiting the free exercise of religion, or abridging the freedom of speech, or the press, or the right of people peaceably to assemble, and petititon to the government for the redress of grievances." The Senate also dropped Madison's favorite amendment, one that prohibited the states from infringing on personal rights. This lack was not corrected until the passage of the fourteenth amendment after the Civil War.

The differences between the Senate and House versions of the amendments were quickly ironed out by a joint committee, which also added a preamble to the bill to explain that the amendments were offered to the states because certain ratification conventions had "expressed a desire . . . that further declaratory and restrictive clauses be added." On October 2, 1789, President Washington sent the proposed amendments to the states.

The first two articles in the twelve were never ratified by a sufficient number of states to make them effective. These called for a change in basis for the apportionment in the lower house as population increased and the compensation of senators and congressmen. Nine of the remaining ten provided for safeguarding the personal rights of citizens; these are truly the Bill of Rights. The tenth covered powers reserved to the states.

Virginia was the first state to start discussion of ratification, and discussed it on and off for two years. New Jersey was the first to ratify, followed by Maryland. North Carolina had joined the union and ratified next, then New Hampshire, South Carolina, Delaware, Pennsylvania, and New York. Rhode Island ratified the Constitution and the amendments almost simultaneously. Meanwhile, Vermont had entered the union and ratified as the tenth state. With fourteen states in the union an eleventh ratification was necessary under the three-fourths rule. Virginia quietly ratified on December 15, 1791, to make the Bill of Rights effective.

It is of interest, although of no importance, that Connecticut, Massachusetts, and Georgia did not ratify the first ten amendments for 150 years. Their ratification was not necessary in 1791. In 1941 they ratified as a gesture during the sesquicentennial celebration of the Bill of Rights.

The fabric was finished, but few, then, expected it to be a very durable piece of cloth. When Franklin was asked what kind of a government the new charter provided, he replied, rather caustically, "A Republic—if you can keep it." At the time, not all Americans were by any means sure that they wanted to keep it. Yet by the early years of the nineteenth century the Constitution had come to be regarded with an almost holy reverence; and it has lasted long enough to become the most venerable written charter of government in history.

Three words in the Constitution have been quoted with particular reverence through the years in political speeches and holiday oratory: *We, the people.* The words are ironic when it is remembered how they came into being. Of course, the Constitution is a covenant between the people of the United States and their government, but this is not the reason that the Framing Fathers opened its preamble with the impressive statement "We, the People of the United States . . ." Until the Constitution reached the Committee of Style it read, "We the people of the states of New Hampshire, Massachusetts, etc." This expressed what the framers were trying to do—draw a charter of govern-

ment for a union of states. But because the document now
provided that this union would become valid when nine
states had ratified, it was obviously impossible to list the
states, because none knew which would ratify. This problem was solved simply by dropping out the names of the
states, none knowing, at the time, how significant this
change would become in the light of later history.

Incidentally, this is not the first American document in
which this phrase was used. When the Five Nations of
Indians drew their treaty, presumably in 1520, they started
it by saying, "We, the people, to form a union, to establish
peace, equity and order . . ."

Britain's famed statesman William Gladstone once said,
"As the British Constitution is the most subtle organism
which has proceeded from progressive history, so the
American Constitution is the most wonderful work ever
struck off at a given time by the brain and purpose of
man." Although this statement may be generally true, it
gives something of a false impression. The Constitution
did not spring forth full-blown like Minerva from the
heads of its fathers. They too were proceeding from progressive history; a very short history, it is true, but their
ideas had historical precedent.

The framers of the Constitution accomplished, basically,
what they had set out to do; they revised the Articles of
Confederation—a very radical revision but nonetheless a
revision. They added an executive to the government, divided the legislature into two parts, defined the judiciary,
and gave Congress the power to levy taxes and to enforce
federal authority, within limits, on the states. But, in the
main, the powers of the new government were largely
identical with the powers of the old. The provisions of the

powers of Congress in the Constitution and in the Articles of Confederation are in some cases the same word for word. Also, much of the federal Constitution is drawn from various state constitutions. In this the constitution of New York state seems to have been used more than any other.

The most remarkable aspect of the Constitution is that it has lasted so long and served so well, with so little change—yet it is not, basically, a very logical charter of government. It could not be, in view of the manner in which it was created. The fifty-five men who met in Philadelphia in 1787 had, as their primary purpose, the solution of certain immediate, practical, problems; things that experience had proved were weaknesses in their present government. These were the things with which they were concerned; not a charter of government that would last through the centuries and provide for all contingencies. Most of their solutions were the result of compromises. A few were so vaguely expressed that they were subject to various interpretations.

No one could have expected the gentlemen at Philadelphia to anticipate changes that would be wrought by such purely technological advances as railroads, electricity, and space exploration. But it is inconceivable that men of the caliber of Madison, Hamilton, Wilson, and others would not have at least discussed certain eventualities had their main concern been to create a logical and consistent charter of government. As a glaring instance, the question of whether a state might dissolve its connection with the union was not even mentioned in all the debate in Philadelphia; it took a long and bloody war to decide that it could not.

They did specify that "This Constitution . . . shall be the supreme law of the land" and provided how this supreme law could be changed or modified by amendment. In 175 years the Constitution has been amended only thirteen times, after the first ten amendments, and most of these later additions involve technicalities. The eleventh amendment modifies the functions of the federal judiciary, the twelfth provides for the election of a Vice-President, the seventeenth changes the manner of electing senators, the twentieth changes the date of inauguration, the twenty-second denies the President a third term, and the twenty-third gives the franchise to citizens of the District of Columbia. The eighteenth and the twenty-first, dealing with prohibition, cancel each other out. This leaves only three subjects of major importance that have been covered by amendments; slavery, women's suffrage, and income tax.

Of the three amendments added as the result of the abolition of slavery—the thirteenth, fourteenth, and fifteenth—the fourteenth has had a much wider interpretation because its "due process" clause has been interpreted to give the central government authority to protect the civil liberties of citizens within the states. The Bill of Rights restricts only the national government—not the state governments—from infringing on the basic rights of citizens.

Yet the Constitution, with these few significant amendments, has served to govern a nation that has grown from 3 million people to almost 200 million people; grown from thirteen states to fifty; progressed from stage coaches to space rockets; moved from a small agricultural society to the world's leading industrial power. This has been possible because the Constitution, within certain broad limits, can progress with the times, can mean what the people, or the government, want it to mean at any given time.

The creation and development of the Department of Agriculture is a case in point. After he retired from the Presidency, Thomas Jefferson organized an agricultural society in Albermarle County, Virginia, and proposed that other counties do likewise and that the societies exchange information. At the time he wrote: "Some have proposed to Congress to incorporate such a society. I am against that because I think that Congress cannot find in all the enumerated powers any which authorizes the act, much less the giving of money to that use." About fifty years later Abraham Lincoln took a different view and signed a bill to create a small federal department that would "collect and disseminate" information among farmers. About seventy-five years later the administration of Franklin D. Roosevelt decided that this department could determine how much of certain crops farmers could plant and exercise jurisdiction over some basic commodity prices. All of this was done, without amendments, based on a progressive reinterpretation of original language of the Constitution.

Another example is road building. The Constitution authorizes Congress to maintain post offices and post roads. In 1806 Congress used this authority to start building the National Pike from Maryland to the Mississippi River. Before it was finished the railroads arrived to carry interstate mails. Work on the National Pike, supported with federal funds, was stopped in 1841, and from that time until 1916 Congress took the attitude that it was not authorized to spend federal money on roads. Then, after the automobile became a reality, Congress decided that it did have the right to build roads and passed the Federal Aid Road Act, from which stems the present system of national highways. Again, it was a matter of reinterpreting the meaning of the Constitution to meet modern contingencies.

There are two particular phrases in the Constitution that have been interpreted to permit the government to keep pace with the progress of our more complex society. One is *To make all laws that are necessary and proper for carrying into execution the foregoing powers.* When John Marshall was Chief Justice of the Supreme Court this was interpreted as the doctrine of "implied powers." For instance, although the Constitutional Convention turned down the proposal to give Congress authority to build canals, the right to "regulate commerce . . . among the several states" has been interpreted as authority to do anything necessary for the best conduct of such commerce. This covers not only such regulatory agencies as the Federal Trade Commission and the Federal Communications Commission, but an entire program of public works involving roads, dams, bridges, electric power sources, and so on.

The most controversial phrase in the Constitution consists of two words: *general welfare.* Considering how careful the framers were to be specific about the powers of government, it is amazing that they used such a vague phrase in Article 1 Section 8 of the document. It is also used in the preamble, as it was in the Articles of Confederation, where it unquestionably applies only to the broad, over-all purpose of union or confederation.

What became Article 1 Section 8 originally read: "The legislature of the United States shall have the power to lay and collect taxes, duties, imposts and excises." It was then proposed that this be modified by adding *to pay the debts and provide for the common defense and the general welfare*. This was accepted unanimously, without discussion. There is no question that most of the framers understood this phrase to apply only to the purposes for which Congress could appropriate money within the framework of its enumerated powers.

This is evident from the fact that, in the document submitted by the Committee of Style, Gouverneur Morris had separated the words *general welfare* from the preceding and following clauses with semicolons, thus intimating that the right of Congress to legislate for the general welfare might be construed as an independent power. This was in accord with Morris's ideas, but it was not the way in which it had been adopted by the convention. In the Constitution as it was finally engrossed the punctuation was removed.

Increasingly, in recent years, this phrase has been interpreted to give Congress the right to pass any legislation that it deems to be for the "general welfare" regardless of whether such legislation comes within the scope of the powers of the government enumerated in the Constitution. Most of the so-called welfare legislation of the past thirty years was possible, without Constitutional amendments, only through such an interpretation of this phrase.

There has always been controversy among men of different political opinion as to the interpretation of the Constitution; and it is very probable that there always will be. Advocates of either side of almost any issue can usually find what they consider support for their point of view in the Constitution. On the face of it, this might seem to be a weakness in a charter of government. But, perhaps, herein lies the basic strength of the Constitution, for it is not a holy document, but a very human one. It was created by men to spell out the basic rights and responsibilities of government to the people and of the people to the government. In the quaint words of William Penn, written in 1682 in his *Frame of Government for Pennsilvania:* "Governments, like clocks, go from the motion men give them; and as governments are made and moved by men, so by them they are ruined too. Wherefore governments rather depend upon men than men upon governments."

Appendix A:
The Constitution
of the United States

WE THE PEOPLE of the United States, in Order to form a more perfect Union, establish Justice, insure domestic Tranquility, provide for the common defence, promote the general Welfare, and secure the Blessings of Liberty to ourselves and our Posterity, do ordain and establish this Constitution for the United States of America.

ARTICLE I

SECTION 1. All legislative Powers herein granted shall be vested in a Congress of the United States, which shall consist of a Senate and House of Representatives.

SECTION 2. The House of Representatives shall be composed of Members chosen every second Year by the People of the several States, and the Electors in each State shall have the Qualifications requisite for Electors of the most numerous Branch of the State Legislature.

No Person shall be a Representative who shall not have attained to the age of twenty five Years, and been seven Years a Citizen of the United States, and who shall not, when elected, be an Inhabitant of that State in which he shall be chosen.

Representatives and direct Taxes shall be apportioned among the several States which may be included within this Union, according to their respective Numbers, which shall be determined by adding to the whole Number of free Persons, including those bound to Service for a Term of Years, and excluding Indians not taxed, three fifths of all other Persons. The actual Enumeration shall be made within three Years after the first Meeting of the Congress of the United States, and within every subsequent Term in ten Years, in such Manner as they shall by Law direct. The Number of Representatives shall not exceed one for every thirty Thousand, but each State shall have at Least one Representative; and until such enumeration shall be made, the State of New Hampshire shall be entitled to chuse three, Massachusetts eight, Rhode-Island and Providence Plantations one, Connecticut five, New-York six, New Jersey four, Pennsylvania eight, Delaware one, Maryland six, Virginia ten, North Carolina five, South Carolina five, and Georgia three.

When vacancies happen in the Representation from any State, the Executive Authority thereof shall issue Writs of Election to fill such Vacancies.

The House of Representatives shall chuse their Speaker and other Officers; and shall have the sole Power of Impeachment.

SECTION 3. The Senate of the United States shall be composed of two Senators from each State, chosen by the Legislature thereof, for six Years; and each Senator shall have one Vote.

Immediately after they shall be assembled in Consequence of the first Election, they shall be divided as equally as may be into three Classes. The Seats of the Senators of the first Class shall be vacated at the Expiration of the second Year, of the second Class at the Expiration of the fourth Year, and of the third Class at the Expiration of the sixth Year, so that one third may be chosen every second Year; and if Vacancies happen by Resignation, or otherwise, during the Recess of the Legislature of any State, the Executive thereof may make temporary Appointments until the next Meeting of the Legislature, which shall then fill such Vacancies.

No Person shall be a Senator who shall not have attained to the Age of thirty Years, and been nine Years a Citizen of the United States, and who shall not, when elected, be an Inhabitant of that State for which he shall be chosen.

The Vice President of the United States shall be President of the Senate, but shall have no Vote, unless they be equally divided.

The Senate shall chuse their other Officers, and also a President pro tempore, in the Absence of the Vice President, or when he shall exercise the Office of President of the United States.

The Senate shall have the sole Power to try all Impeachments. When sitting for that Purpose, they shall be on Oath or Affirmation. When the President of the United States is tried, the Chief Justice shall preside: And no Person shall be convicted without the Concurrence of two thirds of the Members present.

Judgment in Cases of Impeachment shall not extend further than to removal from Office, and disqualification to hold and enjoy any Office of honor, Trust or Profit under the United States: but the Party convicted shall nevertheless be liable and subject to Indictment, Trial, Judgment and Punishment, according to Law.

SECTION 4. The Times, Places and Manner of holding Elections for Senators and Representatives, shall be prescribed in each State by the Legislature thereof; but the Congress may at any time by Law make or alter such Regulations, except as to the Places of chusing Senators.

The Congress shall assemble at least once in every Year, and such Meeting shall be on the first Monday in December, unless they shall by Law appoint a different Day.

SECTION 5. Each House shall be the Judge of the Elections, Returns and Qualifications of its own Members, and a Majority of each shall constitute a Quorum to do Business; but a smaller Number may adjourn from day to day, and may be authorized to compel the attendance of absent Members, in such Manner, and under such Penalties as each House may provide.

Each House may determine the Rules of its Proceedings, punish its Members for Disorderly Behaviour, and, with the Concurrence of two thirds, expel a Member.

Each House shall keep a Journal of its Proceedings, and from time to time publish the same, excepting such Parts as may in their Judgment require Secrecy; and the Yeas and Nays of the Members of either House on any question shall, at the Desire of one fifth of those Present, be entered on the Journal.

Neither House, during the Session of Congress, shall, without the Consent of the other, adjourn for more than three days, nor to any other Place than that in which the two Houses shall be sitting.

SECTION 6. The Senators and Representatives shall receive a Compensation for their Services, to be ascertained by Law, and paid out of the Treasury of the United States. They shall in all Cases, except Treason, Felony and Breach of the Peace, be privileged from Arrest during their Attendance at the Session of their respective Houses, and in going to and returning from the same; and for any Speech or Debate in either House, they shall not be questioned in any other Place.

No Senator or Representative shall, during the Time for which he was elected, be appointed to any civil Office under the Authority of the United States, which shall have been created, or the Emoluments whereof shall have been encreased during such time; and no Person holding any Office under the United States, shall be a member of either House during his Continuance in Office.

SECTION 7. All Bills for raising Revenue shall originate in the House of Representatives; but the Senate may propose or concur with Amendments as on other Bills.

Every Bill which shall have passed the House of Representatives and the Senate, shall, before it becomes a Law, be presented to the President of the United States; If he approve he shall sign it, but if not he shall return it, with his Objections to that House in which it shall have originated, who shall enter the Objections at large on their Journal, and proceed to reconsider it. If after such Reconsideration two thirds of that House shall agree to pass the Bill, it shall be sent, together with the Objections, to the other House, by which it shall likewise be reconsidered, and if approved by two thirds of that House, it shall become a Law. But in all such Cases the Votes of both Houses shall be determined by Yeas and Nays, and the Names of the Persons voting for and against the Bill shall be entered on the Journal of each House respectively. If any Bill shall not be returned by the President within ten Days (Sundays excepted) after it shall have been presented to him, the same shall be a Law, in like Manner as if he had signed it, unless the Congress by their Adjournment prevent its Return, in which Case it shall not be a Law.

Every Order, Resolution, or Vote to which the Concurrence of the Senate and House of Representatives may be necessary (except on a question of Adjournment) shall be presented to the President of the United States; and before the same shall take Effect, shall be approved by him, or being disapproved by him, shall be repassed by two thirds of the Senate and House of Representatives, according to the Rules and Limitations prescribed in the Case of a Bill.

SECTION 8. The Congress shall have Power: To lay and collect Taxes, Duties, Imports and Excises, to pay the Debts and provide for the common Defence and general Welfare of the United States; but all Duties, Imposts and Excises shall be uniform throughout the United States;

To borrow Money on the credit of the United States;

To regulate Commerce with foreign Nations, and among the several States, and with the Indian Tribes;

To establish an uniform Rule of Naturalization, and uniform Laws on the subject of Bankruptcies throughout the United States;

To coin Money, regulate the Value thereof, and of foreign Coin, and fix the Standard of Weights and Measures;

To provide for the Punishment of counterfeiting the Securities and current Coin of the United States;

To establish Post Offices and post Roads;

To promote the Progress of Science and useful Arts, by securing for limited Times to Authors and Inventors the exclusive Right to their respective Writings and Discoveries;

To constitute Tribunals inferior to the supreme Court;

To define and punish Piracies and Felonies committed on the high Seas, and Offences against the Law of Nations;

To declare War, grant Letters of Marque and Reprisal, and make Rules concerning Captures on Land and Water;

To raise and support Armies, but no Appropriation of Money to that Use shall be for a longer Term than two Years;

To provide and maintain a Navy;

To make Rules for the Government and Regulation of the land and naval Forces;

To provide for calling forth the Militia to execute the Laws of the Union, suppress Insurrections and repel Invasions;

To provide for organizing, arming, and disciplining, the Militia, and for governing such Part of them as may be employed in the Service of the United States, reserving to the States respectively, the Appointment of the Officers, and the Authority of training the Militia according to the discipline prescribed by Congress;

To exercise exclusive Legislation in all Cases whatsoever, over such District (not exceeding ten Miles square) as may, by Cession of particular States, and the Acceptance of Congress, become the Seat of the Government of the United States, and to exercise like Authority over all Places purchased by the Consent of the Legislature of the State in which the same shall be, for the Erection of Forts, Magazines, Arsenals dock-Yards, and other needful Buildings;—And

To make all Laws which shall be necessary and proper for carrying into Execution the foregoing Powers, and all other Powers vested by this Constitution in the Government of the United States, or in any Department or Officer thereof.

SECTION 9. The Migration or Importation of such Persons as any of the States now existing shall think proper to admit, shall not be prohibited by the Congress prior to the Year one thousand eight hundred and eight, but a Tax or duty may be imposed on such Importation, not exceeding ten dollars for each Person.

The Privilege of the Writ of Habeas Corpus shall not be suspended, unless when in Cases of Rebellion or Invasion the public Safety may require it.

No Bill of Attainder or ex post facto Law shall be passed.

No Capitation, or other direct, Tax shall be laid, unless in Proportion to the Census or Enumeration herein before directed to be taken.

No Tax or Duty shall be laid on Articles exported from any State.

No Preference shall be given by any Regulation of Commerce or Revenue to the Ports of one State over those of another: nor shall Vessels bound to, or from, one State, be obliged to enter, clear, or pay Duties in another.

No Money shall be drawn from the Treasury, but in Consequence of Appropriations made by Law; and a regular Statement and Account of the Receipts and Expenditures of all public Money shall be published from time to time.

No Title of Nobility shall be granted by the United States: And no Person holding any Office of Profit or Trust under them, shall, without the Consent of the Congress, accept of any present, Emolument, Office, or Title, of any kind whatever, from any King, Prince, or foreign State.

SECTION 10. No State shall enter into any Treaty, Alliance, or Confederation; grant Letters of Marque and Reprisal; coin Money; emit Bills of Credit; make any Thing but gold and silver Coin a Tender in Payment of Debts; pass any Bill of Attainder, ex post facto Law, or Law impairing the Obligation of Contracts, or grant any Title of Nobility.

No State shall, without the Consent of the Congress, lay any Imposts or Duties on Imports or Exports, except what may be absolutely necessary for executing its inspection Laws: and the net Produce of all Duties and Imposts, laid by any State on Imports or Exports, shall be for the Use of the Treasury of the United States; and all such Laws shall be subject to the Revision and Controul of the Congress.

No State shall, without the Consent of Congress, lay any Duty of Tonnage, keep Troops, or Ships of War in time of Peace, enter into any Agreement or Compact with another State, or with a foreign Power, or engage in War, unless actually invaded, or in such imminent Danger as will not admit of delay.

ARTICLE II

SECTION 1. The executive Power shall be vested in a President of the United States of America. He shall hold his Office during the Term of four Years, and, together with the Vice President, chosen for the same Term, be elected, as follows

Each State shall appoint, in such Manner as the Legislature thereof may direct, a Number of Electors, equal to the whole Number of Senators and Representatives to which the State may be entitled in the Congress: but no Senator or Representative, or Person holding an Office of Trust or Profit under the United States, shall be appointed an Elector.

The Electors shall meet in their respective States, and vote by Ballot for two Persons, of whom one at least shall not be an Inhabitant of the same State with themselves. And they shall make a List of all the Persons voted for, and of the Number of Votes for each; which List they shall sign and certify, and transmit sealed to the Seat of the Government of the United States, directed to the President of the Senate. The President of the Senate shall, in the Presence of the Senate and House of Representatives, open all the Certificates, and the Votes shall then be counted. The Person having the greatest Number of Votes shall be the President, if such Number be a Majority of the whole Number of Electors appointed; and if there be more than one who have such Majority, and have an equal Number of Votes, then the House of Representatives shall immediately chuse by Ballot one of them for President; and if no Person have a Majority, then from the five highest on the List the said House shall in like Manner chuse the President. But in chusing the President, the Votes shall be taken by States, the Representation from each State having one Vote; A quorum for this Purpose shall consist of a Member or Members from two thirds of the States, and a Majority of all the States shall be necessary to a Choice. In every Case, after the Choice of the President, the Person having the greatest Number of Votes of the Electors shall be the Vice President. But if there should remain two or more who have equal Votes, the Senate shall chuse from them by Ballot the Vice President.

The Congress may determine the Time of chusing the Electors, and the Day on which they shall give their Votes; which Day shall be the same throughout the United States.

No Person except a natural born Citizen, or a Citizen of the United States, at the time of the Adoption of this Constitution, shall be eligible to the Office of President; neither shall any Person be eligible to that Office who shall not have attained to the Age of thirty five Years, and been fourteen Years a Resident within the United States.

In Case of the Removal of the President from Office, or of

his Death, Resignation, or Inability to discharge the Powers and Duties of the said Office, the Same shall devolve on the Vice President, and the Congress may by Law provide for the Case of Removal, Death, Resignation, or Inability, both of the President and Vice President, declaring what Officer shall then act as President, and such Officer shall act accordingly, until the Disability be removed, or a President shall be elected.

The President shall, at stated Times, receive for his Services, a Compensation, which shall neither be encreased nor diminished during the Period for which he shall have been elected, and he shall not receive within that Period any other Emolument from the United States, or any of them.

Before he enter on the Execution of his Office, he shall take the following Oath or Affirmation:—"I do solemnly swear (or affirm) that I will faithfully execute the Office of President of the United States, and will to the best of my Ability, preserve, protect and defend the Constitution of the United States."

SECTION 2. The President shall be Commander in Chief of the Army and Navy of the United States, and of the Militia of the several States, when called into the actual Service of the United States; he may require the Opinion, in writing, of the principal Officer in each of the executive Departments, upon any Subject relating to the Duties of their respective Offices, and he shall have Power to grant Reprieves and Pardons for Offences against the United States, except in Cases of Impeachment.

He shall have Power, by and with the Advice and Consent of the Senate, to make Treaties, provided two thirds of the Senators present concur; and he shall nominate, and by and with the Advice and Consent of the Senate, shall appoint Ambassadors, other public Ministers and Consuls, Judges of the supreme Court, and all other Officers of the United States, whose Appointments are not herein otherwise provided for, and which shall be established by Law: but the Congress may by Law vest the Appointment of such inferior Officers, as they think proper, in the President alone, in the Courts of Law, or in the Heads of Departments.

The President shall have Power to fill up all Vacancies that may happen during the Recess of the Senate, by granting Commissions which shall expire at the End of their next Session.

SECTION 3. He shall from time to time give to the Congress Information of the State of the Union, and recommend to their Consideration such Measures as he shall judge necessary and expedient; he may, on extraordinary Occasions, convene both Houses, or either of them, and in Case of Disagreement between them, with Respect to the Time of Adjournment, he may adjourn them to such Time as he shall think proper; he shall receive Ambassadors and other public Ministers; he shall take Care that the Laws be faithfully executed, and shall Commission all the Officers of the United States.

SECTION 4. The President. Vice President and all civil Officers of the United States, shall be removed from Office on Impeachment for, and Conviction of, Treason, Bribery, or other high Crimes and Misdemeanors.

ARTICLE III

SECTION 1. The judicial Power of the United States, shall be vested in one supreme Court, and in such inferior Courts as the Congress may from time to time ordain and establish. The Judges, both of the supreme and inferior Courts, shall hold their Offices during good Behaviour, and shall, at stated Times, receive for their Services, a Compensation, which shall not be diminished during their Continuance in Office.

SECTION 2. The judicial Power shall extend to all Cases, in Law and Equity, arising under this Constitution, the Laws of the United States, and Treaties made, or which shall be made, under their Authority;—to all Cases affecting Ambassadors, other public Ministers and Consuls;—to all Cases of admiralty and maritime Jurisdiction;—to Controversies to which the United States shall be a Party;—to Controversies between two or more States;—between a State and Citizens of another State; —between Citizens of different States,—between Citizens of the same State claiming Lands under Grants of different States, and between a State, or the Citizens thereof, and foreign States, Citizens or Subjects.

In all Cases affecting Ambassadors, other public Ministers and Consuls, and those in which a State shall be Party, the supreme Court shall have original Jurisdiction. In all the other Cases before mentioned, the supreme Court shall have appellate Jurisdiction, both as to Law and Fact, with such Exceptions, and under such Regulations as the Congress shall make.

The Trial of all Crimes, except in Cases of Impeachment, shall be by Jury; and such Trial shall be held in the State where the said Crimes shall have been committed; but when not committed within any State, the Trial shall be at such Place or Places as the Congress may by Law have directed.

SECTION 3. Treason against the United States, shall consist only in levying War against them, or in adhering to their Enemies, giving them Aid and Comfort. No Person shall be convicted of Treason unless on the Testimony of two Witnesses to the same overt Act, or on Confession in open Court.

The Congress shall have Power to declare the Punishment of Treason, but no Attainder of Treason shall work Corruption of Blood, or Forfeiture except during the Life of the Person attainted.

ARTICLE IV

SECTION 1. Full Faith and Credit shall be given in each State to the public Acts, Records, and judicial Proceedings of every other State. And the Congress may by general Laws prescribe the Manner in which such Acts, Records and Proceedings shall be proved, and the Effect thereof.

SECTION 2. The Citizens of each State shall be entitled to all Privileges and Immunities of Citizens in the several States.

A Person charged in any State with Treason, Felony, or other Crime, who shall flee from Justice, and be found in another State, shall on Demand of the executive Authority of the State from which he fled, be delivered up, to be removed to the State having Jurisdiction of the Crime.

No Person held to Service or Labour in one State, under the Laws thereof, escaping into another, shall, in Consequence of any Law or Regulation therein, be discharged from such

Service or Labour, but shall be delivered up on Claim of the Party to whom such Service or Labour may be due.

SECTION 3.   New States may be admitted by the Congress into this Union; but no new State shall be formed or erected within the Jurisdiction of any other State; nor any State be formed by the Junction of two or more States, or Parts of States, without the Consent of the Legislatures of the States concerned as well as of the Congress.

The Congress shall have Power to dispose of and make all needful Rules and Regulations respecting the Territory or other Property belonging to the United States; and nothing in this Constitution shall be so construed as to Prejudice any Claims of the United States, or of any particular State.

SECTION 4.   The United States shall guarantee to every State in this Union a Republican Form of Government, and shall protect each of them against Invasion; and on Application of the Legislature, or of the Executive (when the Legislature cannot be convened) against domestic Violence.

ARTICLE V

The Congress, whenever two thirds of both Houses shall deem it necessary, shall propose Amendments to this Constitution, or, on the Application of the Legislatures of two thirds of the several States, shall call a Convention for proposing Amendments, which, in either Case, shall be valid to all Intents and Purposes, as Part of this Constitution, when ratified by the Legislatures of three fourths of the several States, or by Conventions in three fourths thereof, as the one or the other Mode of Ratification may be proposed by the Congress; Provided that no Amendment which may be made prior to the Year One thousand eight hundred and eight shall in any Manner affect the first and fourth Clauses in the Ninth Section of the first Article; and that no State, without is Consent, shall be deprived of its equal Suffrage in the Senate.

ARTICLE VI

All Debts contracted and Engagements entered into, before the Adoption of this Constitution, shall be as valid against the United States under this Constitution, as under the Confederation.

This Constitution, and the Laws of the United States which shall be made in Pursuance thereof; and all Treaties made, or which shall be made, under the Authority of the United States, shall be the supreme Law of the Land; and the Judges in every State shall be bound thereby, any Thing in the Constitution or Laws of any State to the Contrary notwithstanding.

The Senators and Representatives before mentioned, and the Members of the several State Legislatures, and all executive and judicial Officers, both of the United States and of the several States, shall be bound by Oath or Affirmation, to support this Constitution; but no religious Test shall ever be required as a Qualification to any Office or public Trust under the United States.

ARTICLE VII

The Ratification of the Conventions of nine States, shall be sufficient for the Establishment of this Constitution between the States so ratifying the Same.

Done in Convention by the Unanimous Consent of the States present the Seventeenth Day of September in the Year of our Lord one thousand seven hundred and Eighty-seven and of the Independence of the United States of America the Twelfth. In witness whereof We have hereunto subscribed our Names.

Appendix B:
The Bill of Rights

ARTICLE I

Congress shall make no law respecting an establishment of religion, or prohibiting the free exercise thereof; or abridging the freedom of speech, or of the press; or the right of the people peaceably to assemble, and to petition the Government for a redress of grievances.

ARTICLE II

A well regulated Militia, being necessary to the security of a free State, the right of the people to keep and bear Arms, shall not be infringed.

ARTICLE III

No Soldier shall, in time of peace be quartered in any house, without the consent of the Owner, nor in time of war, but in a manner to be prescribed by law.

ARTICLE IV

The right of the people to be secure in their persons, houses, papers, and effects, against unreasonable searches and seizures, shall not be violated, and no Warrants shall issue, but upon probable cause, supported by Oath or affirmation, and particularly describing the place to be searched, and the persons or things to be seized.

ARTICLE V

No person shall be held to answer for a capital, or otherwise infamous crime, unless on a presentment or indicted of a Grand

Jury, except in cases arising in the land or naval forces, or in the Militia, when in actual service in time of War or public danger; nor shall any person be subject for the same offence to be twice put in jeopardy of life or limb; nor shall be compelled in any criminal case to be a witness against himself, nor be deprived of life, liberty, or property, without due process of law; nor shall private property be taken for public use, without just compensation.

ARTICLE VI

In all criminal prosecutions the accused shall enjoy the right to a speedy and public trial, by an impartial jury of the State and district wherein the crime shall have been committed, which district shall have been previously ascertained by law, and to be informed of the nature and cause of the accusation; to be confronted with the witnesses against him; to have compulsory process for obtaining witnesses in his favor, and to have the Assistance of Counsel for his defence.

ARTICLE VII

In suits at common law, where the value in controversy shall exceed twenty dollars, the right of trial by jury shall be preserved, and no fact tried by a jury shall be otherwise reexamined in any Court of the United States, than according to the rules of the common law.

ARTICLE VIII

Excessive bail shall not be required, nor excessive fines imposed, nor cruel and unusual punishments inflicted.

ARTICLE IX

The enumeration in the Constitution, of certain rights, shall not be construed to deny or disparage others retained by the people.

ARTICLE X

The powers not delegated to the United States by the Constitution, nor prohibited by it to the States, are reserved to the States respectively, or to the people.

Index

MA